P. O. Box 17790
Statesboro, GA 30460

W9-CAV-504

# The New Prayer Book Guide
# to Christian Education

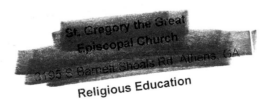

# The New
# *Prayer Book Guide to Christian Education*

Joseph P. Russell, *editor*

COWLEY PUBLICATIONS
Cambridge ✦ Boston
Massachusetts

Originally published in 1983 by the Seabury Press, predecessor in interest to the Domestic and Foreign Missionary Society of the Protestant Episcopal Church in the United States of America.

Published in the United States of America by Cowley Publications, a division of the Society of St. John the Evangelist. No portion of this book may be reproduced, stored in or introduced into a retrieval system, or transmitted, in any form or by any means—including photocopying—without the prior written permission of Cowley Publications, except in the case of brief quotations embodied in critical articles and reviews.

*Library of Congress Cataloging in Publication Data:*
The new prayer book guide to Christian education / Joseph P. Russell—[Rev. ed.]
     p.   cm.
Rev. ed. of: The prayer book guide to Christian education. 1983.
ISBN: 1-56101-121-5 (alk. paper)
1. Christian education—Textbooks—Anglican. 2. Episcopal Church—Book of common prayer.
I. Russell, Joseph P. II. Episcopal Church. The prayer book guide to Christian education.
BX5875.N48 1996
268'.83—dc20                                       95-36350
                                                      CIP

Scripture quotations contained in the text are from *The New Revised Standard Version of the Bible,* copyright 1989, by the Division of Christian Education of the National Council of the Churches of Christ in the United States of America. Psalm quotations are taken from *The Book of Common Prayer,* 1979.

Production of this book was assisted, in part, through a grant given by the Service, Education, and Witness Unit of the Episcopal Church Center.

Edited by Cynthia Shattuck and Vicki Black.
Proofreading assistance provided by Kathleen A. Lewis.
Design and typesetting by Vicki Black.

This book is printed on recycled, acid-free paper and was produced in the United States of America.

*Cowley Publications*
*28 Temple Place*
*Boston, Massachusetts 02111*

# Contents

# Foreword

It has often been said that if you want to know what the Episcopal Church believes theologically, you need to listen to the Episcopal Church at prayer. *The Book of Common Prayer,* with its rites, prayers, catechism, calendar of commemorations, lectionary, and wealth of tradition, carries the weight of theological understanding for the church.

If the Prayer Book is the cornerstone of Anglican theology, then it makes sense to see the Prayer Book as the cornerstone for Christian education in the Episcopal congregation. It was with this understanding in mind that a group of us gathered in 1982 at the invitation of Judith Carlson, then Children's Ministries Officer, at the Episcopal Church Center. Members of this special task force also included Nancy Rayfield, Ruth Cheney, Wilma Smiley, Richard Bower, and myself. Our task was to uncover the treasure of educational objectives and ideas within *The Book of Common Prayer.*

Judith Carlson served as contributor and editor, taking the reams of notes that we produced in our extended session and putting them together in the first edition of *The Prayer Book Guide to Christian Education,* with a foreword by Presiding Bishop John Allin. The response to the book went far beyond our expectations. Today, more than a decade later, I still meet church educators who say that they treasure their one dog-eared extant copy of the guide, and still use it regularly.

It was with pleasure that I received an invitation from Cowley Publications to produce a new edition of *The Prayer Book Guide to Christian Education.* Part of my task has been to update and strengthen certain sections of the first part of the original book concerning the seasons of the church year. The second part of the original book provided brief outlines of the lessons, psalms, and collects of the three-year lectionary. Since this treatment of the lectionary is now available in several other sources, I have provided an entirely new format directed more specifically at the church educator and taking into account the renewal of the catechumenate and the centrality of baptism.

With deep appreciation to the committee who produced the original, *The New Prayer Book Guide to Christian Education* is offered to the church with the prayer that the faith of the church can be embodied in the life of the congregation as it gathers week by week around God's word and sacrament.

*Joseph P. Russell*

# Introduction

## Our Heritage and Textbook

To be an Episcopalian is one way of being a Christian, a Christian with a special set of tools. First among these is *The Book of Common Prayer,* our unique heritage and one we happily share with others. *The Book of Common Prayer* is a manual for worship, and as such it is both the statement of what we believe and our call to ministry. It offers a flexible format for present-day worshiping communities, yet links us securely to our history and traditions; it is a handbook of faith and action. *The Book of Common Prayer* is a primary textbook for Christian education in the Episcopal Church.

In its broadest sense, Christian education is everything and anything happening anywhere that helps the Christian community grow in its life in Jesus Christ and in witness to God. Christian education includes our whole congregational life, everything we do as a community. For children and adults, Christian education includes preaching and hearing, teaching and learning, and sharing in liturgy. Christian education includes what we do outside our church buildings, how we relate to our environment, how we offer our arts, how we share God's story, how we build relationships and grow in love with those around us.

## Who Are the Educators of Christians?

At the ordination of a bishop the candidate is asked, "Will you boldly proclaim and interpret the Gospel of Christ, enlightening the minds and stirring up the conscience of your people?" This responsibility is not solely the bishop's. It is also shared by priests, who are charged by the canons "to be diligent in instruction." At the ordination of a priest, the candidate hears these words that define his or her role in the church: "Now you are called to work as a pastor, priest, and teacher, together with your bishop and fellow presbyters, and to take your share in the councils of the Church."

The directions for Holy Baptism declare that parents and godparents are to be "instructed in their duties to help the new Christians grow in the knowledge and love of God." During the service the entire faith community is asked, "Will you do all in your power to support these persons in their life in Christ?" Then together they accept both personal and corporate responsibility for Christian nurture by affirming and renewing the Baptismal Covenant and by welcoming and receiving the newly baptized into the household of God.

Very clearly, Christian education is a network of mutual responsibility for a ministry in which all persons, both laity and clergy, share. It happens locally, within a congregation or within a family. Growth and learning take place throughout our lives, with possibilities as limitless as God's grace. Teachers and learners become interchangeable as people of all ages discover together to what they are called and to whom they belong.

We are shaped in conscious and in subliminal ways by the liturgy of the church. Faith is formed by the worship experiences shared over a lifetime. That is one reason why the worship experience of the congregation is so crucial. The familiar expression "actions speak louder than words" is true in worship as well. When children, youth, and adults hear God's word proclaimed with power and conviction, they are formed by a community of faith and belief. When they feel a coldness and distance in worship, no number of programs and educational opportunities can cancel out that experience of congregational worship. We must see the liturgy of the church as consistent with what we believe, so that everyone in the faith, young and old, experiences welcome, care, and love.

How liturgy is done has a crucial impact on Christian education. Worship and education must be coordinated and drawn together at every possible juncture. This will take extra time and care, but if educators, musicians, clergy, lay ministers, and others gather around God's word as it unfolds week by week in the lectionary, the stimulation of shared insights will enhance liturgical preparation and lesson planning. Liturgists and educators find themselves as members of a team rather than as isolated individuals struggling for relevance in a lonely pursuit of truth.

## Who Can Use This Book?

This companion guide to *The Book of Common Prayer* is intended to gather in one place information and counsel for living, learning, and engaging the questions of everyday life through the cycle of the church year. Therefore, this book is not just for those who have responsibility for planning or teaching in the church, but for all who share in the life of the Christian community:

- clergy and lay leaders;
- teachers and directors of education;
- lay readers and chalice bearers;
- altar guild members and sacristans;
- organists and music directors;
- writers of parish bulletins and newsletters;
- enquirers of all ages;
- individuals and families who study and pray at home.

This guide is for use along with the Bible and *The Hymnal 1982*. Some of the material may already be familiar, but other resources, including those in the list of "Suggested References and Resources," offer more detailed information when needed. It is hoped that from this raw material programs meeting particular needs can be molded according to local creativity and imagination.

## The Church Year: Framework for Christian Living

We live by many calendars—social, seasonal, civil, personal. The rhythm of our experiences and commitments shapes each of us and provides a context in which we can search for meaning in our personal lives, in our relationships with God and others, in work and play, in joy and pain, in our very living and dying. The church year gives us as Christians this same opportunity. At every point the focus is upon what God has done in Christ for all people in all ages, including our own day. In remembering and celebrating our Christian heritage we are drawn into the salvation story, to encounter and ponder, to proclaim and show forth Jesus Christ, who is "the same yesterday and today and forever" (Heb. 13:8).

Season by season, feast or ordinary day, the church year is like a bright jewel turning in the sunlight whose facets reflect light and hold it for a time so that we may see more clearly within the unity the many splendors, joyful and contemplative, of what it means to share Christ's life on earth. Each repetition of season and feast holds the possibility of our seeing something new, a fresh surprise that can illuminate our understanding and bring us to deeper faith and commitment. The church year gives us, as it has given Christian people throughout the ages, a way to live with Christ so that every year becomes the Year of Our Lord. So we mark our calendars *Anno Domini,* and with "those in every generation in whom Christ has been honored" we "pray that we may have grace to glorify Christ in our own day."

The liturgical year, with its calendar of seasons and commemorations, was really the first curriculum of the church. The familiar pattern of Advent/Christmas/Epiphany and Lent/Holy Week/Easter evolved out of the need of the early church to guide candidates for baptism through the essential narratives and teachings that would form their understanding of God in Christ over the rest of their lives. The Christian calendar, moreover, was developed in part out of the calendar of temple and synagogue as those institutions existed in Jesus' time. Thus the roots of education that is based in lectionary and worship go very deep in our heritage.

## Ways to Use This Guide

The many components of *The Book of Common Prayer* are outlined chronologically in this book, from Advent through the Season after Pentecost, to help you adapt and use them in your own home or congregational setting. The first part of each chapter provides an overview of the entire season, while the second proceeds through the lectionary texts of the season Sunday by Sunday, according to years A, B, and C. The headings described on the following pages are used in each chapter.

### Definition of the Season

Here the season is defined theologically as well as in time and history.

- Mark the season on your calendar and then compare it to vacations, holiday times, and scheduled events in your congregation, community, and world.
- Think about researching how the season has been observed in history and how its meaning has developed today.

### Holy Days in the Season

The major saints' and holy days to be commemorated during the season are listed in this section.

- ◆ Review the complete list of saints' and holy days provided in the calendar at the beginning of *The Book of Common Prayer*.
- ◆ See *Lesser Feasts and Fasts* for prayers, lessons, and biographical information concerning saints in the church calendar. *Lesser Feasts and Fasts* (reissued after each General Convention) introduces the church of today to the great Christians of yesterday. Paging through *Lesser Feasts and Fasts* is like looking through an old family album. Ask yourself, "Who were these people and why are they remembered by the Christian family today?"

### Themes of the Season

This section describes the meaning of the season reflected in the biblical texts specified for Sundays and holy days and in the traditions associated with the season.

- ◆ Choose a theme as a starting point for study.
- ◆ In seasons with several related themes, emphasize one theme this year, another the next.
- ◆ Find out where in your community the theme of the season is being expressed today. Where can the theme be discovered in your daily paper? A bulletin board of clippings, a journal, or a news broadcast could emphasize the theme in your parish.

### Great Words of the Season

Here we see at a glance different words that express various aspects of the themes of the season.

- ◆ Look for the story behind a word.
- ◆ Create a litany or a poem using the words.
- ◆ Feature a "Word of the Week" in the church bulletin or on a poster, or invent crossword puzzles or word games.
- ◆ Ask "What experience have you had of [word]?" "Explain [word] as if to someone from another country, giving examples."
- ◆ Illustrate a word visually with banners, dioramas, or mobiles.

### The Season Through the Eyes of a Child

This section will help begin the "translation" of theological themes for children using simple language and concepts.

- Often children can understand visually or in actions what they cannot express in abstract words. Let them make their own pictures; let them act out ideas ad lib.
- Ask yourself, "In terms of experiences known to these children, how can this idea be explained?"

### Symbols and Traditions of the Season

Symbols represent something with which they are identified, and have meaning when that connection is recognized. Symbols help us to learn about and understand people of other cultures, and to share in their seasonal traditions.

- Use symbols in creative activities. Symbols can be created from all sorts of materials.
- In studying liturgies, identify the symbols and the symbolic actions for clues to learning.
- Find out why some traditions have a long history, while others developed recently. Look at the infinite variety of local variations.
- Traditions are preserved by being practiced. Look for the roots of traditions in your family and in your community.

### Social Justice Themes for the Season

The Baptismal Covenant calls each Christian to "strive for justice and peace among all people, and respect the dignity of every human being." Prophets like Amos and Micah constantly warned the people that social justice and compassion were at the heart of offering worship and praise to God. Because issues of social justice can be controversial, educators and preachers all too often steer clear of focusing on them even when they occur in the lectionary texts. If we are to be faithful to Torah, to the gospel, and to the Baptismal Covenant, themes of social justice need to stand at the center of preaching and teaching.

- Let the lectionary and the Bible shape congregational life. If social justice issues are seen to be a natural outgrowth of biblical concerns for mission and ministry, some of the controversial sting will be removed.
- General social issues that naturally arise could easily become specific and timely for a local educational event and/or an action group.
- Focus a debate or panel discussion on issues of social justice.
- Sponsor a field trip to offer closer involvement with an issue.

### Great Bible Stories for the Season

Bible stories are often found in the season's lectionary and reflect its themes. As noted above under "Through the Eyes of a Child," stories that appear in lectionary texts will be pointed out under the section on the readings (or propers) for that Sunday.

- Stories naturally engage the attention of child and adult alike. Tell the Bible stories that appear in the lectionary texts and are identified in the outline of the propers for each Sunday.
- Choose your own form of telling the story: paraphrasing, showing slides or other illustrations, doing it as a skit or other dramatization, or even by using puppets.
- Choose one character in the reading with whom to identify. "What does it feel like to be that person?" "How would you act or respond?"
- To study the stories of the Bible, read from more than one translation and refer to Bible commentaries.
- Ask questions to aid in your reflection on a Bible passage:
    —What is the writer trying to say?
    —What was the context or situation in which it was written?
    —How is God speaking to us today?

### Great Hymns of the Season

Hymns from *The Hymnal 1982* are included as a reminder of the importance of music and hymnody in our worship and education. *The Hymnal 1982* is, in addition to the Bible and *The Book of Common Prayer,* the church's third major resource book for Christian education.

- Sing familiar songs as well as new ones: singing is an enjoyable way for children and adults to learn about a season.
- Reflect on the words of the hymns, as expressions of the church's faith.
- Study the hymns that are imbedded in the New Testament. For example, Philippians 2:6-11 is considered by many scholars to be a fragment of an early Christian hymn or creed. Trace the biblical origins of hymns. How do the hymns reflect the biblical texts?
- Look at the worship bulletin for the day and discuss why particular hymns were chosen. Ask your church organist or music director to join the discussion.
- Learn the stories that lie behind the hymns. For example, the familiar hymn "Amazing Grace" came out of the painful conversion experience of John Newton, an eighteenth-century slave trader who accepted Christ and later became a priest who worked for the abolition of slavery

in the British Empire. The text takes on a whole new meaning with that story in mind!

- Use *The Episcopal Musician's Handbook* for more complete references and information about hymns.
- Introduce canticles alongside hymns for worship and study. Canticles are songs or chants, other than psalms, with words taken from a biblical text. For example, "The Song of Mary" (BCP 119) is taken from Luke 1:47-55.

### *The Season in* The Book of Common Prayer

This section looks at the season in the context of the Prayer Book and links themes of the season with prayers and services found in *The Book of Common Prayer. The Book of Common Prayer* can be supplemented with *The Book of Occasional Services,* which is issued in succeeding editions after each General Convention and contains a wide variety of services used on an "occasional" basis, such as house blessings and prayers for catechumens.

- Read the services at home, or use them for study. A discussion might consider the form, historical usage, and significant personal impressions of the services. Note how their symbols and biblical images and ideas express the season's meaning.
- Participate in corporate worship whenever possible. Liturgy is *doing.* For example, participate in the Reconciliation of a Penitent and then reflect on the experience by asking, "What have I discovered about sin and reconciliation as a result of my experience of this service?"

### *Living the Season at Home and in the Parish*

This section offers ideas for home and family worship, devotions, and activities. These ideas are intended to help people of all ages participate actively in learning about and expressing the themes of each season.

## The Sundays of the Season

In the second part of each chapter, the following headings are offered to help you gain a quick overview of the lectionary texts for each Sunday in the season.

### Theme of the lections

During the great seasons of the church year, the theme will usually be reflected in all three readings and the appointed psalm. During the Season after Pentecost (often referred to as "Ordinary Time"), two themes will usually be listed. This is because both the gospel of the year (Matthew in Year A, Mark in Year B, and Luke in Year C) and several epistles are read semi-continuously during these months, and therefore any thematic relationship between the gospel and epistle lections is coincidental. The first reading from the Hebrew scriptures is always in thematic harmony with the gospel, and the psalm is a meditative response to the first reading.

### Phrases for highlighting and memorization

One verse or phrase from each lection is included in this section, providing another way of expressing the theme through banners, bulletin covers, or artistic renditions of the focus text. In some cases memorization may be a good way of reinforcing the lesson for the day.

### Key words, ideas, and concepts to explore

As "Great Words" are offered seasonally, so words, ideas, and concepts that unfold in each week's lectionary readings are outlined as well. Here you may want to focus in on one idea, such as the "mountain of the Lord" or "the second coming" in Advent.

### Stories to tell

If a Bible story is a part of one of the readings, it is mentioned here.

### Christian practice and liturgical tradition

Sometimes a biblical text lies behind a particular practice or tradition of the church. An appreciation for history and heritage is enhanced when we begin to see the biblical sources for the worship and life of the church.

### Formation in baptismal discipleship

In this final section, attention is drawn to how the texts need to be embodied in the life of the congregation so that children, youth, and adults are truly formed in the faith. We are formed through our participation in and practice of the Christian life, so that the values and beliefs of the church become our own. In this section, we move from "head to heart."

# *Advent*

## Definition

Advent means "coming" in Latin. Advent is the first season of the church year. It has four Sundays; the first is the Sunday nearest November 30. The last day of Advent is always December 24, the day before Christmas.

## Holy Days in Advent

- St. Andrew the Apostle (November 30);
- St. Thomas the Apostle (December 21).

## Advent Themes

A season of preparation, to prepare the way of the Lord:

- for the Messiah (Savior) promised by God and foretold by the prophets;
- for the expected coming of the baby Jesus, born of Mary at Bethlehem;
- for Christ, the Prince of Peace, who is coming again at the close of this age (called Eschaton) to rule as Lord over the promised kingdom (or reign) of God;
- for each of us to pray the Lord's Prayer with conviction: "*your* kingdom come, *your* will be done." The constant question to ask is: If Jesus revealed God's will and kingdom, how do we as individuals and the church witness to that reality?

## Great Words of Advent

| | |
|---|---|
| Angels (messengers of God) | Coming |
| Annunciation | Deliverance |
| Anticipation | Eschatology (endtimes) |
| Apocalypse | Expectation |

| Fulfillment | Messiah |
|---|---|
| Hope | Peace |
| Judgment | Preparation |
| Kingdom of God | Promise |
| Light of the world | Prophet |
| Longing | Reconciliation |
| Redemption | Waiting |

*Maranatha!* Come, Lord Jesus!

## Advent Through the Eyes of a Child

In Advent, we who are the church:

- ◆ wait for the coming of the baby Jesus whom God gave to us and to all people because God loves us and has made us family;
- ◆ celebrate God's promise to be with us now and always;
- ◆ remember that Jesus will come again in glory and loving power to make all things new;
- ◆ can understand Advent by experiences of waiting, hope, promises, and love in our lives now.

## Symbols and Traditions of Advent

- ◆ Color—purple or blue for preparation, penitence, and royalty;
- ◆ Advent wreath—a green wreath with candles, one for each of the four Sundays;
- ◆ Jesse tree—a tree with symbols of Old Testament prophecies of Jesus' coming; compare the Jesse tree to your own family tree or one about your parish;
- ◆ Empty crèche—awaiting the Christ child;
- ◆ Advent calendar—to count the days to Christmas;
- ◆ Light contrasted with darkness—Jesus is the Light of the world; at the time of Christmas, the days begin to get longer;
- ◆ The *Gloria* and other "glorious hymns"—omitted as we solemnly prepare for Christ's coming;
- ◆ The "O Antiphons"—study the hymn "O come, O come, Emmanuel" with concordance and Bible;
- ◆ An Advent Festival of Lessons and Carols—a traditional English service, found in *The Book of Occasional Services*.

Advent is a time of judgment as we look forward to the coming kingdom and realize the sinfulness of the present age. It is Jesus who reveals the reign of God to the church in every generation. As noted above, the Lord's Prayer leads us to pray that God's will (not ours) be done, "on earth as in heaven." How do these familiar words call us into judgment?

The collects of the Advent season give us a natural way of approaching ethical and social justice issues:

*Advent 1*

"Give us grace to cast away the works of darkness" (BCP 211):
- in personal ethics—things we do as individuals that we are ashamed of when we hold our actions up to the light of Christ;
- in business and political ethics—looking at business practices that fail to measure up to the demands of the coming kingdom.

*Advent 2 and 3*

"Who sent your messengers the prophets to preach repentance and prepare the way for our salvation" (BCP 211). Social issues raised by Amos and Isaiah provide an outline of contemporary issues:
- corruption in public affairs;
- oppression of peoples, especially the poor, through selfish, self-indulgent lifestyles;
- failing to carry out justice for the good of the people, and to care for the poor, the widow, the orphan, and the disadvantaged;
- practicing empty formalism in religion, concentrating on self-fulfillment rather than the word of the Lord, listening to false prophets who mislead the people;
- relying on military power for security—the arms race;
- seeking wealth by acquiring lands and acquisitions to the detriment of others (corporate ethical responsibility).

*Advent 4*

"Jesus Christ, at his coming, may find in us a mansion prepared for himself" (BCP 212):
- whatever we do personally and publicly will be done in a way that prepares the world for the coming of Christ.

# Great Bible Stories for Advent

### The Prophecies in Isaiah
- The Lord's sign to the House of David (Isaiah 7:10-17);
- The stem of Jesse and the peaceable kingdom (Isaiah 11:1-10);
- Comfort, O comfort my people (Isaiah 40:1-11).

### Elizabeth
- Mary visiting her cousin (Luke 1:39-56);
- The birth of John the Baptist is promised (Luke 1:5-25).

### John the Baptist
- Baptizing in the river Jordan (Matthew 3:1-12; Mark 1:1-8; Luke 3:7-18);
- Messengers sent from John (Matthew 11:2-11).

### Mary
- The Annunciation (Luke 1:26-56);
- Joseph's dream (Matthew 1:18-25).

# Great Hymns of Advent

Advent hymns 53-76, including:
- Come, thou long-expected Jesus (Hymn 66);
- O come, O come, Emmanuel (Hymn 56).

# Advent in *The Book of Common Prayer*

### Prayers and Thanksgivings
- Eucharistic Prayer B emphasizes the Incarnation (BCP 367-369);
- Collects 6 and 7 (BCP 395) conclude the Prayers of the People with Advent themes.

### A Service with Advent Themes
- Order of Worship for the Evening (BCP 109-114).

## Living the Advent Season at Home and in the Parish

- ◆ Make an Advent calendar.
- ◆ Start a collection of food, clothes, or toys in preparation for sharing Christmas love with someone who is needy.
- ◆ Try some creative writing (a poem or story) on an Advent theme—hope or waiting or light, for example. Mary was waiting (Luke 1:26-38); what is it that you are waiting for? Or discuss why hope is an Advent theme and what a message of hope might be for you.
- ◆ Make an Advent capsule (like a time capsule) to tell the children and adults of your parish twenty-five years from this Advent what is important to you today. Include news items that may be offered in a service with the Prayers of the People.
- ◆ Express through visual arts (banners, bulletin boards, murals) some of the prophecies about the expected Messiah. What do they tell us about Jesus and the kingdom of God?
- ◆ Talk about the dreams you may have as you contemplate the coming of the fullness of God's reign. Share the beautiful poetry of hope in passages such as Revelation 21:1-6. What imagery and poetry could we use to describe God's intentions for the coming day based on what we know of Jesus and the great men and women of the Bible who pointed to God's way?

# *The Sundays of Advent*

# ◆ ◆ Year A ◆ ◆

## The First Sunday of Advent, Year A

Lections: Isaiah 2:1-5; Psalm 122; Romans 13:8-14; Matthew 24:37-44

### *Theme of the lections*

The day will come when God's wisdom and presence will be fully revealed. It will be a time of both tremendous hope and promise, but it will also be a time of judgment. God's people must live in readiness for that great day to come.

*Phrases for highlighting and memorization*
- "They shall beat their swords into plowshares, and their spears into pruning hooks." (Isa. 2:4b)
- "I was glad when they said to me, 'Let us go to the house of the LORD.'" (Psalm 122:1)
- "Love does no wrong to a neighbor, therefore, love is the fulfilling of the law." (Rom. 13:10)
- "Keep awake therefore, for you do not know on what day your Lord is coming." (Matt. 24:42)

*Key words, ideas, and concepts to explore*
- mountain of the Lord (Jerusalem or Mount Zion);
- seeking world peace;
- salvation;
- readiness for judgment;
- the Day of the Lord (sometimes referred to as the "Second Coming"; see Acts 1:11; 1 Cor. 15:23; Heb. 9:28; Rev. 1:7).

*Christian practice and liturgical tradition*
- The "memorial acclamation" at the eucharist expresses the Advent theme in one sentence: "Christ will come again."
- "Swords into plowshares" is a theme often cited by groups working for peaceful solutions to the world's problems, including the Episcopal Peace Fellowship.

*Formation in baptismal discipleship*
Christians are called to live expectantly. The good news of Christ's coming again is balanced with the understanding that God comes in judgment. Part of living expectantly is to know that all that is hidden will be revealed.

The season of Advent is a time when the church is called to prepare individuals for baptism on the First Sunday after the Epiphany, the Baptism of our Lord. In Advent, those preparing for their baptism (and their parents and sponsors) are offered a glimpse of God's ultimate vision for creation and humanity. They are challenged to set life goals around that vision. Advent invites the church to dream of what God's will being done fully "on earth as in heaven" might mean in light of Jesus' words and acts.

# The Second Sunday of Advent, Year A

Lections: Isaiah 1:1-10; Psalm 72:1-8; Romans 15:4-13; Matthew 3:1-12

### Theme of the lections
John the Baptist proclaims the coming of Jesus and calls people into repentance through baptism.

### Phrases for highlighting and memorization
- "They will not hurt or destroy on all my holy mountain; for the earth will be full of the knowledge of the LORD as the waters cover the sea." (Isa. 11:9)
- "He shall defend the needy among the people; he shall rescue the poor and crush the oppressor." (Psalm 72:4)
- "For whatever was written in former days was written for our instruction, so that by steadfastness and by the encouragement of the scriptures we might have hope." (Rom. 15:4)
- "I baptize you with water for repentance, but one who is more powerful than I is coming after me; I am not worthy to carry his sandals. He will baptize you with the Holy Spirit and fire." (Matt. 3:11)

### Key words, ideas, and concepts to explore
- baptism;
- Jesse (the Jesse tree);
- Spirit of the Lord;
- the Day of the Lord ushering in a time of peace;
- circumcision as a mark of the covenant;
- John the Baptist;
- repentance;
- preparing the way of the Lord;
- baptism with the Holy Spirit;
- harvest practices of biblical times.

### Stories to tell
- The story of John the Baptist, including the narrative details from the gospel of Luke (Luke 1:5-80).

### Christian practice and liturgical tradition
- The beautiful imagery of all creation being at peace (Isaiah 11) has inspired poets and artists for generations.

• Today's gospel text helps to define the sacrament of baptism. John baptized with water for repentance; Jesus came to baptize with the Holy Spirit and fire. At baptism, the priest anoints the new Christian and says, "*N.*, you are sealed by the Holy Spirit in Baptism and marked as Christ's own forever" (BCP 308).

### Formation in baptismal discipleship

The call to defend the weakest of society and to stand for social justice is inherent in scripture, and therefore must be an integral part of preparing persons for baptism, confirmation, reaffirmation, or reception.

## The Third Sunday of Advent, Year A

Lections: Isaiah 35:1-10; Psalm 146:4-9; James 5:7-10; Matthew 11:2-11

### Theme of the lections

The promised day of God is dawning. John is the herald of that day. Jesus proclaimed the kingdom of God by everything he said and did.

### Phrases for highlighting and memorization

• "Then the eyes of the blind shall be opened, and the ears of the deaf unstopped." (Isa. 35:5)
• "[God] gives justice to those who are oppressed, and food to those who hunger." (Psalm 146:6)
• "You also must be patient. Strengthen your hearts, for the coming of the Lord is near." (James 5:8)
• "Go and tell John what you hear and see: the blind receive their sight, the lame walk, the lepers are cleansed, the deaf hear, the dead are raised, and the poor have good news brought to them." (Matt. 11:4b-5)

### Key words, ideas, and concepts to explore

• John the Baptist;
• the Day of the Lord inaugurates a time of peace;
• the coming of the Lord (or "Second Coming");
• messenger;
• preparing the way.

### Stories to tell

• The story of John the Baptist continues this Sunday;

- The stories of Jesus that lie behind his statement to John's disciples, such as healing a paralyzed man (Mark 2:1-12) and restoring a girl to life (Luke 8:40-42, 49-56).

### Christian practice and liturgical tradition
- We pray for God's kingdom to come every time we pray the Lord's Prayer.

### Formation in baptismal discipleship
The Baptismal Covenant provides the vision for the baptized:

> Will you continue in the apostles' teaching…persevere in resisting evil…proclaim by word and example the Good News of God in Christ…seek and serve Christ in all persons…strive for justice and peace among all people? (BCP 304-305)

It is in living out this covenant call that the church responds to the question raised by John, "Are you the one who is to come, or are we to wait for another?" (Matt. 11:3). The first reading and the gospel lection lie behind the church's call to be deeply involved in the ministry of service and justice. The church continues in the role of Jesus, pointing out God's coming reign in such actions.

## The Fourth Sunday of Advent, Year A
Lections: Isaiah 7:10-17; Psalm 24:1-7; Romans 1:1-7; Matthew 1:18-25

### Theme of the lections
Jesus' imminent birth is proclaimed in the scriptures. His continued presence in the world is proclaimed by the church today.

### Phrases for highlighting and memorization
- "Therefore the Lord himself will give you a sign. Look, the young woman is with child and shall bear a son, and shall name him Immanuel." (Isa. 7:14)
- "Lift up your heads, O gates; lift them high, O everlasting doors; and the King of glory shall come in." (Psalm 24:7)
- "The gospel concerning [God's] Son, who was descended from David according to the flesh and was declared to be Son of God with power according to the spirit of holiness by resurrection from the dead, Jesus Christ our Lord." (Rom. 1:3-4)

◆ "She will bear a son, and you are to name him Jesus, for he will save his people from their sins." (Matt. 1:21)

### Key words, ideas, and concepts to explore
- ◆ Sheol;
- ◆ gospel;
- ◆ prophets;
- ◆ significance of King David;
- ◆ Mary and Joseph;
- ◆ significance of the name "Jesus."

### Stories to tell
- ◆ The stories from Matthew and Luke leading up to Jesus' birth.

### Christian practice and liturgical tradition
- ◆ Hymn 436, "Lift up your heads, ye mighty gates," reflects the psalm appointed for today.

### Formation in baptismal discipleship
The role of the Christian congregation, and the individual Christian, is to reflect the presence of God in the world today. From the Fourth Sunday of Advent through the Feast of the Epiphany, the church celebrates the Incarnation; God is present "in the flesh" of human life. God meets us in the midst of our human struggle. The collect for the First Sunday after Christmas Day expresses this idea well:

*Almighty God, you have poured upon us the new light of your incarnate Word: Grant that this light, enkindled in our hearts, may shine forth in our lives....* (BCP 213)

♦ ♦ **Year B** ♦ ♦

## The First Sunday of Advent, Year B

Lections: Isaiah 64:1-9a; Psalm 80:1-7; 1 Corinthians 1:1-9; Mark 13:(24-32) 33-37

### Theme of the lections

The day will come when God's wisdom and presence will be fully revealed. It will be a time of both tremendous hope and promise, but it will also be a time of judgment. God's people must live in readiness for that great day to come.

### Phrases for highlighting and memorization

- ◆ "Do not be exceedingly angry, O LORD, and do not remember iniquity forever." (Isa. 64:9a)
- ◆ "Restore us, O God of hosts; show the light of your countenance and we shall be saved." (Psalm 80:3)
- ◆ "He will also strengthen you to the end, so that you may be blameless on the day of our Lord Jesus Christ." (1 Cor. 1:8)
- ◆ "Beware, keep alert; for you do not know when the time will come." (Mark 13:33)

### Key words, ideas, and concepts to explore

- ◆ judgment;
- ◆ grace;
- ◆ spiritual gifts;
- ◆ "day of our Lord Jesus Christ";
- ◆ being watchful.

### Formation in baptismal discipleship

See Advent 1, Year A. The church has been given the grace and gifts to minister in the name of Christ.

# The Second Sunday of Advent, Year B

Lections: Isaiah 40:1-11; Psalm 85:7-13; 2 Peter 3:8-15a, 18; Mark 1:1-8

### Theme of the lections

John the Baptist announces the coming of the long expected day pointed to in the Hebrew scriptures. The "good tidings" of Isaiah 40 become the "good news" announced in the opening words of the gospel according to Mark. Repentance is a part of accepting that good news.

### Phrases for highlighting and memorization

- "A voice cries out: 'In the wilderness prepare the way of the LORD, make straight in the desert a highway for our God.'" (Isa. 40:3)
- "Righteousness shall go before him, and peace shall be a pathway for his feet." (Psalm 85:13)
- "Therefore, beloved, while you are waiting for these things, strive to be found by him at peace, without spot or blemish; and regard the patience of our Lord as salvation." (2 Peter 3:14-15a)
- "And people from the whole Judean countryside and all the people of Jerusalem were going out to him, and were baptized by him in the river Jordan, confessing their sins." (Mark 1:5)

### Key words, ideas, and concepts to explore

- God is like a shepherd;
- new heavens and a new earth;
- gospel;
- baptism;
- apocalyptic literature;
- baptism with the Holy Spirit.

### Stories to tell

- The story of John the Baptist, including the narrative details from the gospel of Luke (Luke 1:5-80).

### Christian practice and liturgical tradition

- The beautiful text from Isaiah may be familiar from Handel's *Messiah*.
- The origin of the word "gospel" comes from the Isaiah text and from Mark's opening words. "Gospel" means "good news."

### Formation in baptismal discipleship
The radical call for repentance informs the preparation given for those preparing for their baptism (see also Luke 3:1-20).

## The Third Sunday of Advent, Year B
Lections: Isaiah 65:17-25; Psalm 126 or Canticle 15; 1 Thessalonians 5:(12-15) 16-28; John 1:6-8, 19-28

### Theme of the lections
The promised day of God is dawning. John is the herald of that day.

### Phrases for highlighting and memorization
- "For I am about to create new heavens and a new earth; the former things shall not be remembered or come to mind." (Isa. 65:17)
- "The LORD has done great things for us, and we are glad indeed." (Psalm 126:4)
- "He has filled the hungry with good things, and the rich he has sent away empty." (Canticle 15, "The Song of Mary")
- "Rejoice always, pray without ceasing, give thanks in all circumstances; for this is the will of God in Christ Jesus for you." (1 Thess. 5:16-17)
- "[John] came as a witness to testify to the light, so that all might believe through him." (John 1:7)

### Key words, ideas, and concepts to explore
- John the Baptist;
- the vision of the perfect Day of the Lord that is to come;
- prayer;
- the "coming of our Lord Jesus Christ" (or the "Second Coming");
- Christ (Messiah);
- role of Elijah (from Malachi 4:5);
- baptism.

### Stories to tell
- John the Baptist (continued from Advent 2).

### Christian practice and liturgical tradition
- The tradition of lighting Advent candles comes from references to the light and to the dawning of a new day expressed in this Sunday's gospel lection.

### Formation in baptismal discipleship
Those preparing for their baptism on the First Sunday after the Epiphany (The Baptism of our Lord) need to look carefully at the beautiful poetic description of God's coming day of perfect peace. Using their own words and imagery, how would candidates for baptism (or their parents and sponsors) describe God's intentions fully realized in the day that is coming? How can the church live in such a way that the dream is expressed in the lives of the people?

## The Fourth Sunday of Advent, Year B
Lections: 2 Samuel 7:4, 8-16; Psalm 132:8-15; Romans 16:25-27; Luke 1:26-38

### Theme of the lections
God's promise of favor to the house of David and to the people is fulfilled in Jesus. A mystery is revealed. The promise now includes the Gentiles.

### Phrases for highlighting and memorization
- "He shall build a house for my name, and I will establish the throne of his kingdom forever." (2 Sam. 7:13)
- "The LORD has sworn an oath to David; in truth, he will not break it: 'A son, the fruit of your body will I set upon your throne.'" (Psalm 132:11-12)
- "...the revelation of the mystery that was kept secret for long ages but is now disclosed, and through the prophetic writings is made known to all the Gentiles." (Rom. 16:25b-26a)
- "He will be great, and will be called the Son of the Most High, and the Lord God will give to him the throne of his ancestor David." (Luke 1:32)

### Key words, ideas, and concepts to explore
- significance of the house of David;
- the "revelation of the mystery";
- gospel;

- Son of God;
- Elizabeth, mother of John the Baptist.

### Stories to tell
- The stories from Matthew and Luke leading up to Jesus' birth.

### Christian practice and liturgical tradition
- The references in the liturgy of the church to the House of David and the honor given to King David find their significance in today's lections.
- The honor given Mary stems from her willingness to respond to God's call.

### Formation in baptismal discipleship
See Advent 4, Year A above.

## ✦ ✦ Year C ✦ ✦

## The First Sunday of Advent, Year C
Lections: Zechariah 14:4-9; Psalm 50:1-6; 1 Thessalonians 3:9-13; Luke 21:25-31

### Theme of the lections
God's day is coming when all the world will know the power and authority of God. Poetry best describes this mystery. The whole earth, in earthquake and other natural phenomena, will proclaim that great day.

### Phrases for highlighting and memorization
- "On that day living waters shall flow out from Jerusalem, half of them to the eastern sea and half of them to the western sea; it shall continue in summer as in winter." (Zech. 14:8)
- "Our God will come and will not keep silence." (Psalm 50:3a)
- "And may the Lord make you increase and abound in love for one another and for all, just as we abound in love for you." (1 Thess. 3:12)
- "Heaven and earth will pass away, but my words will not pass away." (Luke 21:33)

### Key words, ideas, and concepts to explore
- the Day of the Lord;
- judgment;
- "Son of man coming in a cloud";
- the kingdom of God.

### Christian practice and liturgical tradition
- The baptismal theme of "living waters" is found in the first reading. The gospel of John picks up this emphasis on "living waters" (see John 4:10 and 7:38). In some churches, moving or "living" waters flow through the baptismal font, symbolizing the texts we hear this week.

### Formation in baptismal discipleship
See Advent 1, Year A above.


## The Second Sunday of Advent, Year C
Lections: Baruch 5:1-9; Psalm 126; Philippians 1:1-11; Luke 3:1-6

### Theme of the lections
John the Baptist proclaims the coming of Jesus and calls people into repentance through baptism.

### Phrases for highlighting and memorization
- "Arise, O Jerusalem, stand upon the height; look toward the east, and see your children gathered from west and east at the word of the Holy One, rejoicing that God has remembered them." (Baruch 5:5)
- "When the LORD restored the fortunes of Zion, then were we like those who dream." (Psalm 126:1)
- "I am confident of this, that the one who began a good work among you will bring it to completion by the day of Jesus Christ." (Phil. 1:6)
- "He went into all the region around the Jordan, proclaiming a baptism of repentance for the forgiveness of sins." (Luke 3:3)

### Key words, ideas, and concepts to explore
- Timothy, a disciple of Paul;
- John the Baptist;
- a baptism of repentance;
- forgiveness of sins.

### Stories to tell
- The story of John the Baptist.

### Christian practice and liturgical tradition
- Repentance is a part of conversion; it means to turn in a new direction. In the baptismal rite candidates first reject evil and then turn to accept Jesus Christ as Savior and Lord. In the early church and in the Orthodox tradition today, those to be baptized faced west as they denounced evil and then turned around to face east as they accepted Jesus.

### Formation in baptismal discipleship
The radical call for repentance guides the preparation given for those preparing for their baptism. This week's gospel lection needs to be read in the context of next week's gospel, Luke 3:7-18.

## The Third Sunday of Advent, Year C

Lections: Zephaniah 3:14-20; Psalm 85:7-13 or Canticle 9; Philippians 4:4-7 (8-9); Luke 3:7-18

### Theme of the lections
God's new day is dawning in Jesus. It will be a day in which God's compassion for the weak and oppressed is fully realized. In the meantime, Christians must act in accordance with God's intentions for the kingdom.

### Phrases for highlighting and memorization
- "I will deal with all your oppressors at that time. And I will save the lame and gather the outcast, and I will change their shame into praise." (Zeph. 3:19)
- "I will listen to what the LORD God is saying, for he is speaking peace to his faithful people and to those who turn their hearts to him." (Psalm 85:8)
- "And on that day you shall say, Give thanks to the Lord and call upon his Name." (Canticle 9, "The First Song of Isaiah")
- "Rejoice in the Lord always; again, I will say, Rejoice." (Phil. 4:4)
- "Whoever has two coats must share with anyone who has none; and whoever has food must do likewise." (Luke 3:11)

*Key words, ideas, and concepts to explore*
- the coming Day of the Lord (or "Second Coming");
- John the Baptist;
- repentance;
- ethics of the gospel;
- the Baptismal Covenant calls us to service and justice.

*Stories to tell*
- John the Baptist (continued from Advent 2).

*Christian practice and liturgical tradition*
- The Advent season combines a sense of joyous hope in God's coming with power in the fullness of time, as well as the radical call for repentance (a life turned around) that goes with the vision. Hope and judgment are the twin themes of the Advent season.

*Formation in baptismal discipleship*
The radical lifestyle of the repentant Christian is outlined in the words of John the Baptist heard in the gospel. Those preparing for their baptism on the First Sunday after the Epiphany (The Baptism of our Lord), and the parents and sponsors of candidates, must discern how those radical words will affect them in their covenant life.

## The Fourth Sunday of Advent, Year C

Lections: Micah 5:2-4; Psalm 80:1-7; Hebrews 10:5-10; Luke 1:39-49 (50-56)

*Theme of the lections*
God's promise of favor to the house of David and to the people is fulfilled in Jesus. A mystery is revealed. The promise now includes the Gentiles.

*Phrases for highlighting and memorization*
- "But you, O Bethlehem of Ephrathah, who are one of the little clans of Judah, from you shall come forth for me one who is to rule in Israel, whose origin is from of old, from ancient days." (Micah 5:2)
- "Restore us, O God of hosts; show the light of your countenance, and we shall be saved." (Psalm 80:3)
- "And it is by God's will that we have been sanctified through the offering of the body of Jesus Christ once for all." (Heb. 10:10)

- "My soul magnifies the Lord, and my spirit rejoices in God my Savior." (Luke 1:47)

### Key words, ideas, and concepts to explore
- Bethlehem as the birthplace of Jesus;
- the meeting of Mary and Elizabeth.

### Stories to tell
- The stories from Matthew and Luke leading up to Jesus' birth.

### Christian practice and liturgical tradition
- "The Song of Mary" (*The Magnificat*), often said or sung at Evening Prayer, is included in the gospel lection. (Notice the radical nature of Mary's song: the poor shall be raised up and the powerful will be brought down.)

### Formation in baptismal discipleship
See Advent 4, Year A above.

# *Christmas*

## Definition

December 25 is the feast day on which we celebrate the birth of our Lord Jesus Christ. Our word "Christmas" comes from the old English *christmasse* (Christ's Mass). In ancient calendars the feast was set close to the winter solstice, when the sun returned light to the world.

## Holy Days in the **Christmas Season**

- St. Stephen, Deacon and Martyr (December 26);
- St. John, Apostle and Evangelist (December 27);
- The Holy Innocents (December 28);
- The Holy Name of Our Lord Jesus Christ (January 1).

## Christmas Themes

Christ is born!

- In the birth of Jesus, God gave us the greatest gift by becoming a human being and dwelling among us. Jesus is truly God and truly human—the Incarnation is God's plan for reconciling and redeeming his people.
- It is important to emphasize at Christmas that the great celebration is more than a remembrance of the birth of the baby Jesus. It is a joyful proclamation of the Incarnation. God is known in the flesh of human life. People who knew Jesus realized with awe and wonder that to be with Jesus was to be with God. They knew God in their flesh and blood relationship with Jesus. The good news of Christmas is that through the power of the Holy Spirit we can still know God in the flesh of human life and relationship. God is not a distant creative power. God is as

close as the love that binds one to another in a way that points beyond the human encounter to the divine revelation.

- In Christ we, who are made in the image of God, behold the dignity of our human nature. Because Christ came to bring salvation (healing, "salving"), we have hope and assurance of sharing his life both now and always.

## Great Words of Christmas

| | |
|---|---|
| Angels | Nativity |
| Annunciation | New light |
| Celebration | Reconciliation |
| Fulfillment | Redeemer |
| Incarnation | Savior |
| Judge | |

## Christmas Through the Eyes of a Child

At Christmas, we who are the church:

- welcome Jesus and joyfully celebrate his birth;
- give thanks for God's greatest gift of love to us, the Son, Jesus Christ.

## Symbols and Traditions of Christmas

- Color—white for festival and joy;
- Angels—they rejoiced at Jesus' birth;
- Candles—Jesus is the Light of the world;
- Chrismons—symbols about Jesus that are used as tree ornaments, such as stars, candles, mangers, crosses, and shepherds' crooks;
- Crèche (manger scene)—to celebrate the uniqueness of each season, the three magi (wisemen) are not placed in the crèche until the Feast of the Epiphany;
- Evergreen garlands and wreaths (holly, laurel, mistletoe)—for everlasting life;
- Gifts—to share and show love as God has done;
- St. Nicholas/Santa Claus;
- Sheep and shepherds;
- Star;

◆A Festival of Lessons and Carols—a traditional English Christmas service (see *The Book of Occasional Services*).

## Great Bible Stories for Christmas

◆The birth and childhood of Jesus (Luke 2:1-40);
◆The flight into Egypt (Matthew 2:1-15).

## Great Hymns of Christmas

Christmas hymns 77-115, including:
◆Break forth, O beauteous heavenly light (Hymn 91);
◆What child is this (Hymn 115);
◆All glory be to God on high (metrical setting of the *Gloria in excelsis*) (Hymn 421).

## Christmas in *The Book of Common Prayer*

### Prayers and Thanksgivings
◆Eucharistic Prayer B with its reference to the Incarnation is especially appropriate (BCP 367-69).

### Services with Christmas Themes
◆The service of A Thanksgiving for the Birth or Adoption of a Child (BCP 439-445) expresses the wonder of birth and new life. Note the phrase "whoever receives a little child in the name of Christ receives Christ himself" (BCP 443), which reinforces the incarnational theme.

## Living the Christmas Season at Home and in the Parish

◆Families and parishes develop their own traditions for celebrating Jesus' birth. These often include gifts for others, such as clothing, toys, food, or money for persons in need. Gift-giving reflects the joy of God's gift to us; gifts are expressions of God's love shared between people.
◆Neighborhood caroling expresses the call to proclaim the gospel to the world.

- Small trimmed Christmas trees can be made and shared with people who are ill or homebound.
- The *posada* (meaning "inn" in Spanish) is a Latin American tradition in which a procession with figures of Mary and Joseph goes from house to house (or room to room in a home or church) looking for a place of shelter. Sometimes the procession begins nine days before Christmas, which can give it Advent's flavor of expectation. When the "inn" is reached, the innkeeper asks a series of questions before he lets them enter: "Who is knocking?"; "Where have you come from?"; "What do you want here?" After entering the "inn," the figures are brought to the manger. On Christmas Eve the figure of the Christ Child is added, and a celebration with singing and dancing and feasting may follow. The *posada* dramatizes acceptance of the Christ Child in our lives and hearts.
- Candles can be made and burned during the Christmas season, perhaps every night until Twelfth Night. Doorways and walks can be lined with *luminarias,* according to a custom begun in the southwestern United States. These candles, placed on a bed of sand inside brown paper bags, give off an amber glow. Fold down the top of an ordinary small grocery bag about two inches to make it stay open. Place a household candle firmly into the two-inch bed of sand at the bottom of the bag. Lighted at dusk and placed two or three feet apart along lawns or steps, the candles will burn gently for several hours and snuff out when they burn down to the sand base.
- Make a Christingle—an orange decorated with a lighted candle, raisins, and nuts. The orange represents the world, a red ribbon tied around the equator is the Blood of Christ, and the raisins and nuts are the fruits of the earth. The candle is the Light of the World. Christingles—a Moravian custom—might be shared as gifts or lighted from the Christ candle at church or at home. They could be lighted at the end of a service and carried, symbolically, out into the world.

# The Days of Christmas

## ◆ ◆ Years A, B, and C ◆ ◆

## Christmas Day, All Years

Lections: *Christmas Day I:* Isaiah 9:2-4, 6-7; Psalm 96:1-4, 11-12; Titus 2:11-14; Luke 2:1-14 (15-20). *Christmas Day II:* Isaiah 62:6-7, 10-12; Psalm 97:1-4, 11-12; Titus 3:4-7; Luke 2:(1-14) 15-20. *Christmas Day III:* Isaiah 52:7-10; Psalm 98:1-6; Hebrews 1:1-12; John 1:1-14

### *Theme of the lections*

God came in Jesus of Nazareth to reveal the power of God's love and healing. In the birth of Jesus we realize that God shares life with us intimately. We meet God "in the flesh" of human struggle and most especially in the midst of human love. Christmas celebrates the incarnation of God; God "in the flesh of" human life. (*Carne* comes from the Latin for meat or flesh.)

### *Phrases for highlighting and memorization*

- ◆ "For a child has been born for us, a son given to us; authority rests upon his shoulders; and he is named Wonderful Counselor, Mighty God, Everlasting Father, Prince of Peace." (Isa. 9:6)
- ◆ "Shout with joy to the LORD, all you lands; lift up your voice, rejoice, and sing." (Psalm 98:5)
- ◆ "For the grace of God has appeared, bringing salvation to all." (Titus 2:11)
- ◆ "She gave birth to her firstborn son and wrapped him in bands of cloth, and laid him in a manger, because there was no place for them in the inn." (Luke 2:7)

### *Key words, ideas, and concepts to explore*

- ◆ Christian hope;
- ◆ expectation;
- ◆ highway-building as a metaphor of hope;
- ◆ the role of sentinels in biblical times;
- ◆ salvation;
- ◆ incarnation;

- grace;
- royal courtroom imagery as descriptive of Jesus' relationship with God the Father.

### Stories to tell
- The story of the birth of Jesus in Luke's gospel. (Note that the story of the visit of the magi in Matthew's gospel is a story associated with the Feast of the Epiphany, rather than Christmas Day.)

### Christian practice and liturgical tradition
- Christmas pageants are a way of participating in the wonderful story of Jesus' birth.
- The candlelight service at midnight on Christmas Eve reflects the awe and wonder of the angels' visit to the shepherds at night.

### Formation in baptismal discipleship
Luke's account of Jesus being placed in a manger at his birth because there was no room in the inn serves as a constant reminder to the Christian that God identifies with the weak, the poor, and the outcast.


## The First Sunday after Christmas, All Years
Lections: Isaiah 61:10–62:3; Psalm 147:13-21; Galatians 3:23-25, 4:4-7; John 1:1-18

### Theme of the lections
God came in Jesus fully to reveal God's love and forgiveness to all.

### Phrases for highlighting and memorization
- "I will greatly rejoice in the LORD, my whole being shall exult in my God; for he has clothed me with the garments of salvation, he has covered me with the robe of righteousness." (Isa. 61:10a)
- "[God] sends out his command to the earth, and his word runs very swiftly." (Psalm 147:16)
- "But when the fullness of time had come, God sent his Son, born of a woman, born under the law, in order to redeem those who were under the law, so that we might receive adoption as children." (Gal. 4:4-5)
- "The Word became flesh and lived among us, and we have seen his glory, the glory as of a father's only son, full of grace and truth." (John 1:14)

*Key words, ideas, and concepts to explore*
- incarnation;
- *Logos* (Word);
- clothing as metaphor of joy.

*Christian practice and liturgical tradition*
- The wearing of vestments reflects the reading from Isaiah: "he has clothed me with the garments of salvation." In the early church, those who were baptized were given new white garments to wear as a sign of their redeemed relationship with God and the church. Later, the vesting of the priest became associated with being clothed with "the robe of righteousness."
- Though technically Christmas is not a season, since the Sundays are numbered after Christmas, the tradition of the "twelve days of Christmas" is familiar partly from the well-known carol. Twelfth Night, the night before the Feast of the Epiphany, traditionally ends the Christmas "season."

## The Feast of the Holy Name (January 1), All Years

Lections: Exodus 34:1-8; Psalm 8; Romans 1:1-7 or Philippians 2:9-13; Luke 2:15-21

*Theme of the lections*
God's identity is revealed as "merciful and gracious" (Exod. 34:6). Jesus' name has significance: it is the Greek form of the Hebrew name Joshua, meaning "God saves."

*Phrases for highlighting and memorization*
- "The LORD, the LORD, a God merciful and gracious, slow to anger, and abounding in steadfast love and faithfulness." (Exod. 34:6b)
- "O Lord our Governor, how exalted is your Name in all the world!" (Psalm 8:1)
- "The gospel concerning his Son, who was descended from David according to the flesh and was declared to be Son of God with power according to the spirit of holiness by resurrection from the dead, Jesus Christ our Lord." (Rom. 1:3-4)
- "After eight days had passed, it was time to circumcise the child; and he was called Jesus, the name given by the angel before he was conceived in the womb." (Luke 2:21)

### Key words, ideas, and concepts to explore
- significance of Mt. Sinai;
- God's steadfast love and mercy;
- gospel;
- the importance of names;
- covenant and circumcision.

### Stories to tell
- The story of the naming of Jesus.

### Christian practice and liturgical tradition
- The naming of the person being baptized is an important element in the baptismal rite, as in scripture: "You shall be called by a new name that the mouth of the Lord will give" (Isaiah 62:2). In some traditions a child was literally named at baptism and given the name of a Christian saint. Whether or not the name is given at baptism, one's given name takes on new significance as one is adopted into the family of Christ.
- A Thanksgiving for the Birth or Adoption of a Child (BCP 439-445) comes from the ancient traditions of naming and dedicating expressed in the gospel text.

## The Second Sunday after Christmas, All Years

Lections: Jeremiah 31:7-14; Psalm 84:1-8; Ephesians 1:3-6, 15-19a; Matthew 2:13-15, 19-23 or Luke 2:41-52 or Matthew 2:1-12.

### Theme of the lections
The Holy Family flees to Egypt (Matt. 2:13-15, 19-23);
The boy Jesus in the temple (Luke 2:41-52);
The visit of the magi (Matt. 2:1-12).

### Phrases for highlighting and memorization
- "See, I am going to bring them from the land of the north, and gather them from the farthest parts of the earth, among them the blind and the lame, those with child and those in labor, together; a great company, they shall return here." (Jer. 31:8)
- "Happy are the people whose strength is in you! whose hearts are set on the pilgrims' way." (Psalm 84:4)

- "He destined us for adoption as his children through Jesus Christ, according to the good pleasure of his will." (Eph. 1:5)
- "There he made his home in a town called Nazareth, so that what had been spoken through the prophets might be fulfilled, 'He will be called a Nazorean.'" (Matt. 2:23)

### Key words, ideas, and concepts to explore
- adoption as a metaphor of our relationship with God;
- "glorious inheritance";
- Egypt;
- the temple in Jerusalem.

### Stories to tell
- The story in Matthew of the Holy Family fleeing to Egypt;
- The story in Luke of Jesus as a boy visiting the temple;
- The story in Matthew of the visit of the magi.

### Christian practice and liturgical tradition
The adoption language associated with baptism comes from the reading from Ephesians heard this week. See also:

> All praise and thanks to you, most merciful Father, for adopting us as your own children, for incorporating us into your holy Church. (BCP 311)

# *Epiphany*

## Definition

The Feast of the Epiphany, or Manifestation (revelation) of Christ to the Gentiles, is observed on January 6. Epiphany comes from a Greek word meaning "showing forth, appearance, manifestation, revelation." The Feast of the Epiphany proclaims the good news that Jesus revealed God to all humanity.

At Christmas the church celebrates the birth of Jesus, when God entered fully into the human experience. The Feast of the Epiphany takes the Christmas proclamation a step further, when the divine revelation in Jesus was revealed to the world as the magi came from the East.

The eve of the Feast of the Epiphany (Twelfth Night) marks the end of the Christmas celebration. The Epiphany is followed by a period of "Sundays after the Epiphany"; the length of the Epiphany season varies in length from four to nine Sundays, depending on the date of Easter that year.

## Holy Days Following the Feast of the Epiphany

- The Baptism of our Lord (The First Sunday after the Epiphany);
- The Confession of St. Peter the Apostle (January 18);
- The Conversion of St. Paul the Apostle (January 25);
- The Presentation of Our Lord Jesus Christ in the Temple, or Candlemas (February 2).

## Epiphany Themes

- Manifestation (revelation) of Christ to the whole world. When we see Christ we are seeing God.

- Epiphany is a time for remembering the recognition of Jesus as God by many people, among them the magi, John the Baptist, Jesus' disciples, and Christians in every age, including our own.
- Epiphany is a time for rededicating ourselves to our own ministries and our missionary task—to continue the spread of Jesus' light in the world.
- In Epiphany we remember Christ's baptism and our own. Just as the disciples were called, we received our calling or vocation as Christians through our baptism. The theme of discipleship is the initial focus in the readings for the Sundays after the Epiphany.
- Epiphany is a time for remembering the signs of Jesus that revealed his presence to the people, as in the first miracle at Cana and in the healing miracles. Healing and the anointing of the sick are important themes of the Sundays after the Epiphany.

## Great Words of Epiphany

| | |
|---|---|
| Apostle | Magi (wisemen) |
| Baptism | Ministry |
| Calling | Miracle |
| Conversion | Mission |
| Covenant | Outreach |
| Disciple | Revelation |
| Discipleship | Shining star |
| Gifts and treasures | Showing forth |
| Light | Sign |

## Epiphany Through the Eyes of a Child

What Jesus did and said helps us to know who God is and what God is doing for us:

- Jesus called his friends to be with him and to help him in his work;
- Jesus came for all the people of the world;
- Jesus is like a light, helping us to see better;
- We are baptized into God's family, the church.

## Symbols and Traditions of Epiphany

- Colors—white, the festival color, for the Feast of the Epiphany and the days up to and including the next Sunday, which is the Feast of the Baptism of our Lord; green for the weeks after the Epiphany, the color of the ongoing life of the church.
- The "Feast of Lights" emphasizes the theme of the Light of the World, the True Light. Candlelight services are often held in cathedrals and parish churches on the Feast of the Epiphany.
- Baptisms are celebrated on the feast of Jesus' baptism, the First Sunday after the Epiphany.
- The magi or three wisemen—Matthew's gospel (Matt. 2:1-12) tells of magi (people who studied the movement of the stars to interpret their meaning) who came from the east, following a special star and bringing gifts to the child Jesus. They were Gentiles, not Jews, and they worshiped him. The story of the magi that we know is grounded in legends that came out of the Middle Ages and described them as kings named Melchior, Caspar, and Balthazar.
- The gifts of the magi (as described in Matthew):
  —*Gold* for royalty, wealth, the kingship of Christ;
  —*Frankincense,* made of gum from an Asian and African tree. It may be burned to produce aromatic smoke used in worship, and symbolizes divinity and prayer;
  —*Myrrh,* a bitter resin used in ancient times to anoint bodies before burial; a symbol of suffering and death, foretelling Christ's giving of self through death.
- A single star to recalls the manifestation of Christ to the world;
- Candlemas (from Candle Mass), on February 2, takes its name from the candles carried at the celebration of the Presentation of Christ in the Temple (see *The Book of Occasional Services*). It celebrates a ritual of Jewish law related to first-born sons that Joseph and Mary carried out (Luke 2:21-40). Luke's gospel tells how Simeon and Anna, devout Jews, honored the infant Jesus as the promised Messiah.

## Social Justice Themes for Epiphany

### Epiphany 1: The Baptism of our Lord

The collect for this day asks: "Grant that all who are baptized into his name may keep the covenant they have made" (BCP 214). The

Baptismal Covenant calls Christians to strive for justice and peace among all people, and to respect the dignity of every human being (BCP 305).

*Epiphany 6*
The collect for this Sunday affirms that "in keeping your commandments we may please [God] both in will and deed" (BCP 216). Six of the Ten Commandments, which summarize the 613 commandments of the Torah, remind us that to honor God is to love others as we love ourselves. Many of the commandments of the Torah deal with proper treatment of the poor, the stranger, and the disadvantaged in society, as well as ethical business practices.

Jesus' "new Law" outlined in the Sermon on the Mount calls the Christian to an even higher standard:
- reconciliation in all relationships, including sexual ones;
- truthfulness in business, personal, and political matters;
- justice and respect for human rights;
- love for all people, even those perceived to be enemies.

## Great Bible Stories for Epiphany

- Moses and the burning bush (Exod. 3:1-10) provides a story of God's revelation to Moses and later to the Hebrew people with both words and actions.
- The three traditional stories associated with the Epiphany:
  —The visit of the magi (Matt. 2:1-12);
  —The baptism of Jesus (Matt. 3:13-17; Mark 1:9-11; Luke 3:21-22; John 1:29-34);
  —The marriage in Cana (John 2:1-11).
- The calling of the disciples:
  —The first disciples (Matt. 4:18-22; Mark 1:16-20; Luke 5:1-11; John 1:35-51 and 21:1-8);
  —Names of the Twelve (Matt. 10:1-4; Mark 3:13-19; Luke 6:12-16);
  —Matthew (Matt. 9:9-13; Mark 2:13-17; Luke 5:27-32);
  —Philip (John 1:43-51).

## Great Hymns of Epiphany

Epiphany hymns 116-139, including:

- We three kings of Orient are (Hymn 128);
- What star is this, with beams so bright (Hymn 124).

## Epiphany in *The Book of Common Prayer*

### *Prayers and Thanksgivings*

- Eucharistic Prayer B (BCP 367-369);
- Thanksgiving for the Mission of the Church (BCP 838);
- Collect for the Mission of the Church (BCP 257);
- Collect: Of a Missionary (BCP 247);
- Thanksgiving for the Gift of a Child (BCP 841).

### *Services with Epiphany Themes*

- Holy Baptism (BCP 299-310);
- Confirmation (BCP 413-419);
- A Form of Commitment to Christian Service (BCP 420-421);
- Ordination—Bishop, Priest, Deacon (BCP 512-551);
- Celebration of a New Ministry (BCP 559-564);
- An Order of Worship for the Evening (BCP 109-114) expresses the theme of light.

## Living the Epiphany Season at Home and in the Parish

- Be particularly aware of baptisms on the feast of the Baptism of our Lord on the First Sunday after the Epiphany. We all celebrate birthdays; in the church it is appropriate to celebrate and talk about the anniversary of our baptism. (Those baptized as infants may need to ask their parents or godparents about their baptisms.) If there are baptisms on this Sunday, make gifts for those to be baptized (such as a baptismal candle or baptismal day memory booklet). Discuss and plan ways that everyone in the faith community can support the newly baptized.
- Have a procession of the three kings, robed and bearing their gifts to the crèche as part of the liturgy on the Feast of the Epiphany.

◆ A parish party could include an Epiphany cake, caroling, and a visit from the three kings bearing gifts. The magi are an important focus among many Latin American and Spanish-speaking groups. In Spain, Costa Rica, and Puerto Rico, children fill their shoes with straw for the magi's camels, later finding presents in their place given by the kings, a reminder of the gifts to the Christ Child.

# The Sundays of Epiphany

## The Epiphany, All Years

Lections: Isaiah 60:1-6, 9; Psalm 72:1-2, 10-17; Ephesians 3:1-12; Matthew 2:1-12

### Theme of the lections
The significance of Jesus' birth is revealed to the world beyond Judea.

### Phrases for highlighting and memorization
- ◆ "Arise, shine; for your light has come, and the glory of the LORD has risen upon you." (Isa. 60:1)
- ◆ "May his Name remain for ever and be established as long as the sun endures; may all the nations bless themselves in him and call him blessed." (Psalm 72:17)
- ◆ "Although I am the very least of all the saints, this grace was given me to bring to the Gentiles the news of the boundless riches of Christ, and to make everyone see what is the plan of the mystery hidden for ages in God who created all things." (Eph. 3:8-9)
- ◆ "On entering the house, they saw the child with Mary his mother; and they knelt down and paid him homage." (Matt. 2:11a)

### Key words, ideas, and concepts to explore
- ◆ mysteries hidden that are now revealed;
- ◆ "eternal purpose";
- ◆ hope for the restoration of Judea;
- ◆ the significance of gold, frankincense, and myrrh.

### Stories to tell
- ◆ The story of the visit of the magi.

### Christian practice and liturgical tradition

◆ The magi join the nativity scene at the crèche on the Feast of the Epiphany.

### Formation in baptismal discipleship

Christians are to continue "revealing the mystery" to the world. As God appeared in Jesus, so God appears through the Holy Spirit in the people of God who are the church.

## The First Sunday after the Epiphany: The Baptism of our Lord, All Years

Lections: Isaiah 42:1-9; Psalm 89:20-29, Acts 10:34-38; Matthew 3:13-17 (Year A), Mark 1:7-11 (Year B), Luke 3:15-16, 21-22 (Year C)

### Theme of the lections

The baptism of Jesus.

### Phrases for highlighting and memorization

◆ "Here is my servant, whom I uphold, my chosen, in whom my soul delights; I have put my spirit upon him; he will bring forth justice to the nations." (Isa. 42:1)

◆ "My hand will hold him fast and my arm will make him strong." (Psalm 89:21)

◆ "That message spread throughout Judea, beginning in Galilee after the baptism that John announced: how God anointed Jesus of Nazareth with the Holy Spirit and with power; how he went about doing good and healing all who were oppressed by the devil, for God was with him." (Acts 10:37-38)

◆ "And a voice came from heaven, 'You are my Son, the Beloved; with you I am well pleased.'" (Mark 1:11)

### Key words, ideas, and concepts to share

◆ justice;
◆ servant;
◆ Jesus as "Lord of all";
◆ baptism with water and the Holy Spirit;
◆ role of John the Baptist.

### Stories to tell
- Jesus' baptism;
- Jesus' temptations in the wilderness.

### Christian practice and liturgical tradition
- This Sunday is one of the five most appropriate times for baptism in the church (see BCP 312).

### Formation in baptismal discipleship
The words of calling and anointing for ministry heard in connection with Jesus' baptism are the words that frame the church's understanding of the ministry of all the baptized today: "You are my...Beloved; with you I am well pleased."


◆ ◆ **Year A** ◆ ◆


## The Second Sunday after the Epiphany, Year A
Lections: Isaiah 49:1-7; Psalm 40:1-10; 1 Corinthians 1:1-9; John 1:29-41

### Theme of the lections
Responding to God's call to be a "light to the nations."
- *Epistle:* Paul greets the church at Corinth with thanksgiving. (This Sunday begins a serialized reading of 1 Corinthians 1–4; therefore, the epistle reading will not usually be in thematic harmony with the Old Testament, psalm, and gospel lections.)

### Phrases for highlighting and memorization
- "I will give you as a light to the nations, that my salvation may reach to the end of the earth." (Isa. 49:6b)
- "In the roll of the book it is written concerning me: 'I love to do your will, O my God; your law is deep in my heart.'" (Psalm 40:9)
- "God is faithful; by him you were called into the fellowship of his Son, Jesus Christ our Lord." (1 Cor. 1:9)
- "When Jesus turned and saw them following, he said to them, 'What are you looking for?' They said to him, 'Rabbi' (which translated means Teacher), 'where are you staying?' He said to them, 'Come and see.'" (John 1:38-39a)

### Key words, ideas, and concepts to explore

- "light to the nations";
- servant;
- salvation;
- redeemer;
- overview of 1 Corinthians;
- Lamb of God;
- rabbi;
- the apostles Andrew and Simon Peter.

### Stories to tell

- During the early Sundays after the Epiphany, we hear the stories of Jesus calling his disciples. Explore these stories from all three years of the lectionary.

### Christian practice and liturgical tradition

- The baptismal rite includes elements of being called that reflect Jesus' call to the first disciples: "I present *N.* to receive the sacrament of baptism...Do you renounce Satan...Do you turn to Jesus?"

### Formation in baptismal discipleship

Christians see their baptism as a calling into discipleship. Christ calls people into servanthood today as the first disciples were called on the lakeshore and in the counting house.

## The Third Sunday after the Epiphany, Year A

Lections. Amos 3:1-8; Psalm 139:1-11; 1 Corinthians 1:10-17; Matthew 4:12-23

### Theme of the lections

The calling of the disciples, yesterday and today.

- *Epistle:* Paul castigates the church at Corinth for its divisiveness.

### Phrases for highlighting and memorization

- "Surely the Lord GOD does nothing, without revealing his secret to his servants the prophets." (Amos 3:7)
- "LORD, you have searched me out and known me; you know my sitting down and my rising up; you discern my thoughts from afar." (Psalm 139:1)

- "Now I appeal to you, brothers and sisters, by the name of our Lord Jesus Christ, that all of you be in agreement and that there be no divisions among you, but that you be united in the same mind and the same purpose." (1 Cor. 1:10)
- "And he said to them, 'Follow me, and I will make you fish for people.' Immediately they left their nets and followed him." (Matt. 4:19-20)

### Key words, ideas, and concepts to explore
- the prophet Amos;
- the role of prophets;
- divisions in the church;
- repentance;
- the calling of the disciples.

### Stories to tell
- The stories of Jesus calling his disciples continue from Epiphany 2.

### Christian practice and liturgical tradition
See Epiphany 2, Year A.

### Formation in baptismal discipleship
See Epiphany 2, Year A.

## The Fourth Sunday after the Epiphany, Year A
Lections: Micah 6:1-8; Psalm 37:1-6; 1 Corinthians 1:(18-25) 26-31; Matthew 5:1-12

### Theme of the lections
The Sermon on the Mount: God's word is revealed. God's way is proclaimed.
- *Epistle:* God's wisdom versus the world's wisdom.

### Phrases for highlighting and memorization
- "He has told you, O mortal, what is good; and what does the LORD require of you but to do justice, and to love kindness, and to walk humbly with your God?" (Micah 6:8)
- "Commit your way to the LORD and put your trust in him, and he will bring it to pass." (Psalm 37:5)

- "Consider your own call, brothers and sisters: not many of you were wise by human standards, not many were powerful, not many were of noble birth." (1 Cor. 1:26)
- "When Jesus saw the crowds, he went up the mountain; and after he sat down, his disciples came to him." (Matt. 5:1)

### Key words, ideas, and concepts to explore

- doing justice;
- courtroom proceedings to express God's anger at the nation;
- God's wisdom;
- the Sermon on the Mount.

### Christian practice and liturgical tradition

- The powerful words of Micah are reflected in the call for justice in the Baptismal Covenant:

    *"Will you strive for justice and peace among all people, and respect the dignity of every human being?"* (BCP 305)

### Formation in baptismal discipleship

Worship is an act in which the Christian assembly envisions the reign of God in word and sacrament. That is, the values of God's reign are enacted in the ancient pattern of the worship service. ("He has told you, O mortal, what is good...to do justice, and to love kindness, and to walk humbly with your God.")

- We gather in God's name.
- We hear God's radical Word.
- We respond in prayer and thanksgiving.
- We offer ourselves to God (the offertory).
- We share a foretaste of the heavenly banquet (communion).
- We go forth to love and serve.

## The Fifth Sunday after the Epiphany, Year A

Lections: Habakkuk 3:2-6, 17-19; Psalm 27:1-7, 1 Corinthians 2:1-11; Matthew 5:13-20

### Theme of the lections

The Sermon on the Mount: God's people are to give witness to God's grace and power by leading righteous lives.

- *Epistle:* God's wisdom stands in contrast to human wisdom.

### Phrases for highlighting and memorization

- ◆ "Yet I will rejoice in the LORD; I will exult in the God of my salvation." (Hab. 3:18)
- ◆ "The LORD is my light and my salvation; whom then shall I fear? The LORD is the strength of my life; of whom then shall I be afraid?" (Psalm 27:1)
- ◆ "But we speak God's wisdom, secret and hidden, which God decreed before the ages for our glory." (1 Cor. 2:7)
- ◆ "In the same way, let your light shine before others, so that they may see your good works and give glory to your Father in heaven." (Matt. 5:16)

### Key words, ideas, and concepts to explore

- ◆ God's wisdom;
- ◆ the Holy Spirit as the revealer of God's wisdom;
- ◆ salt of the earth and light of the world;
- ◆ God's law (Torah);
- ◆ role of the scribes and Pharisees;
- ◆ the Sermon on the Mount.

### Christian practice and liturgical tradition

- ◆ The tradition of giving candles as a gift at the time of baptism symbolizes the role of the baptized to be lights to the world.

### Formation in baptismal discipleship

Light and darkness are frequent themes in the Bible and Prayer Book. Ministry is bringing Christ's light into the world in the daily life of each Christian and in the corporate witness of the church.

## The Sixth Sunday after the Epiphany, Year A

Lections: Ecclesiasticus 15:11-20; Psalm 119:9-16; 1 Corinthians 3:1-9; Matthew 5:21-24, 27-30, 33-37

### Theme of the lections

The Sermon on the Mount: Jesus' commandments call for a profound commitment, leading the Christian to witness to a distinctive way of life.

- ◆ *Epistle:* Paul castigates the Corinthians for their divisive behavior.

### Phrases for highlighting and memorization

- "Before each person are life and death, and whichever one chooses will be given." (Ecclesiasticus 15:17)
- "My delight is in your statutes; I will not forget your word." (Psalm 119:16)
- "For as long as there is jealousy and quarreling among you, are you not of the flesh, and behaving according to human inclinations?" (1 Cor. 3:3b)
- "So when you are offering your gift at the altar, if you remember that your brother or sister has something against you, leave your gift there before the altar and go; first be reconciled to your brother or sister, and then come and offer your gift." (Matt. 5:23-24)

### Key words, ideas, and concepts to explore

- freedom to choose;
- conflicts within the church;
- the Sermon on the Mount;
- the higher law of Jesus.

### Christian practice and liturgical tradition

- The Collect for Purity (BCP 355) reflects the words from the reading from Ecclesiasticus: "[God] is mighty in power and sees everything; his eyes are on those who fear him, and he knows every human action."
- The offertory at the eucharist continues the ancient temple practice of offering gifts at the altar as an act of commitment to and reconciliation with God.
- The passing of the peace at the eucharist expresses the command of Jesus to leave one's gift at the altar and be reconciled with one's brother and sister and then offer the gift. Since it follows the confession and absolution, the peace is an acting out of the need to forgive as we have been forgiven.

### Formation in baptismal discipleship

The church must take seriously the call for unity and peace within the Body of Christ. Harsh judgments and enmity have no place in the congregation.

## The Seventh Sunday after the Epiphany, Year A

Lections: Leviticus 19:1-2, 9-18; Psalm 71:16-24; 1 Corinthians 3:10-11, 16-23; Matthew 5:38-48

### Theme of the lections

The Sermon on the Mount: our covenant with God calls us to live a life of justice and compassion that surpasses expected behavior.

- *Epistle:* Each Christian is to live as a temple of God.

### Phrases for highlighting and memorization

- "You shall be holy, for I the LORD your God am holy." (Lev. 19:2b)
- "O God, you have taught me since I was young, and to this day I tell of your wonderful works." (Psalm 71:17)
- "Do you not know that you are God's temple and that God's Spirit dwells in you?" (1 Cor. 3:16)
- "Be perfect, therefore, as your heavenly Father is perfect." (Matt. 5:48)

### Key words, ideas, and concepts to explore

- temple of God;
- covenant;
- justice;
- compassion;
- the Sermon on the Mount.

### Formation in baptismal discipleship

The Baptismal Covenant stresses the need to "seek and serve Christ in all persons" and to "strive for justice and peace among all people" (BCP 305). A congregation living out the biblical and baptismal covenant imperative will be constantly exploring issues of justice and compassion. Throughout history the church has stood for justice and compassion in society, out of response to the biblical imperative to be holy as God is holy (Lev. 19:2).

# The Eighth Sunday after the Epiphany, Year A

Lections: Isaiah 49:8-18; Psalm 62:6-14; 1 Corinthians 4:1-5 (6-7) 8-13; Matthew 6:24-34

### Theme of the lections
The Sermon on the Mount: the vision of the kingdom of God.
- *Epistle:* Paul defends his leadership before the Corinthians.

### Phrases for highlighting and memorization
- "See, I have inscribed you on the palms of my hands; your walls are continually before me." (Isa. 49:16)
- "In God is my safety and my honor; God is my strong rock and my refuge." (Psalm 62:8)
- "Think of us in this way, as servants of Christ and stewards of God's mysteries." (1 Cor. 4:1)
- "But strive first for the kingdom of God and his righteousness, and all these things will be given to you as well." (Matt. 6:33)

### Key words, ideas, and concepts to explore
- God's motherly love (Isa. 49:15);
- steward;
- "mysteries of God";
- righteousness;
- mammon;
- the Sermon on the Mount.

### Christian practice and liturgical tradition
- The Daily Office from the Prayer Book expresses the call to live each moment in thanksgiving and praise. The service of Morning Prayer opens with words calling the congregation to praise: "Lord, open our lips. And our mouth shall proclaim your praise" (BCP 80).
- The Lenten customs of living more simply and exercising self-control reflect Jesus' words about setting priorities in life.

### Formation in baptismal discipleship
Today's gospel is a vivid statement about the values and lifestyle of the Christian congregation and each baptized member of the Body of Christ.

# The Last Sunday after the Epiphany, Year A

Lections: Exodus 24:12 (13-14) 15-18; Psalm 99; Philippians 3:7-14; Matthew 17:1-9

### Theme of the lections
The Transfiguration of our Lord.
- *Epistle:* There is nothing more important than knowing Christ.

### Phrases for highlighting and memorization
- "The glory of the LORD settled on Mount Sinai, and the cloud covered it for six days; on the seventh day he called to Moses out of the cloud." (Exod. 24:16)
- "Proclaim the greatness of the Lord our God and worship him upon his holy hill." (Psalm 99:9)
- "I press on toward the goal for the prize of the heavenly call of God in Christ Jesus." (Phil. 3:14)
- "And he was transfigured before them, and his face shone like the sun, and his clothes became dazzling white." (Matt. 17:2)

### Key words, ideas, and concepts to explore
- transfiguration;
- resurrection;
- the role of Moses and Elijah in the Hebrew scriptures;
- Mount Sinai.

### Stories to tell
- The story of Moses on the mountain;
- The story of Jesus' transfiguration.

### Christian practice and liturgical tradition
- The Sundays after the Epiphany are framed by both the Feast of the Epiphany, with its star in the heavens, and Jesus' face shining like the sun at the Transfiguration. The light of God's revelation in Jesus becomes clearer in the ensuing weeks as disciples are called and the word is proclaimed.

### Formation in baptismal discipleship
Each Sunday Christians gather "on the mountain top" in the assembly for the revelation of God so that we can see more clearly the way of Christ in our lives.

## The Second Sunday after the Epiphany, Year B

Lections: 1 Samuel 3:1-10 (11-20); Psalm 63:1-8; 1 Corinthians 6:11b-20; John 1:43-51

### Theme of the lections

Responding to God's call to be a "light to the nations."

♦ *Epistle:* Through baptism, Christians become the sacred temples of the Holy Spirit. (This Sunday begins a serialized reading of 1 Corinthians 6–9 and 2 Corinthians 1–3; therefore, the epistle reading will not usually be in thematic harmony with the Old Testament, psalm, and gospel lections.)

### Phrases for highlighting and memorization

♦ "Now the LORD came and stood there, calling as before, 'Samuel! Samuel!' And Samuel said, 'Speak, for your servant is listening.'" (1 Sam. 3:10)

♦ "O God, you are my God; eagerly I seek you; my soul thirsts for you, my flesh faints for you, as in a barren and dry land where there is no water." (Psalm 63:1)

♦ "Do you not know that your body is a temple of the Holy Spirit within you, which you have from God, and that you are not your own?" (1 Cor. 6:19)

♦ "The next day Jesus decided to go to Galilee. He found Philip and said to him, 'Follow me.'" (John 1:43)

### Key words, ideas, and concepts to explore

♦ the temple and the ark of God;
♦ our bodies are "temples of the Holy Spirit";
♦ baptism as being sanctified and washed;
♦ the disciples Philip, Andrew, Simon Peter, and Nathanael;
♦ the title "rabbi";
♦ overview of Paul's correspondence to the Corinthians.

### Stories to tell

♦ During the early Sundays after the Epiphany, we hear the stories of Jesus calling his disciples. Explore these stories from all three years of the lectionary.

### Christian practice and liturgical tradition

◆ The baptismal rite includes elements of being called that reflect Jesus' call to the first disciples: "I present *N.* to receive the sacrament of baptism...Do you renounce Satan...Do you turn to Jesus?"

### Formation in baptismal discipleship

Christians see their baptism as a calling into discipleship. Christ calls people into servanthood today as the first disciples were called on the lakeshore and in the counting house.

## The Third Sunday after the Epiphany, Year B

Lections: Jeremiah 3:21–4:2; Psalm 130; 1 Corinthians 7:17-23; Mark 1:14-20

### Theme of the lections

The calling of the disciples, yesterday and today.

◆ *Epistle:* Baptism does not mean changing one's status in life.

### Phrases for highlighting and memorization

◆ "Truly in the LORD our God is the salvation of Israel." (Jer. 3:23b)
◆ "Out of the depths have I called to you, O LORD; LORD, hear my voice; let your ears consider well the voice of my supplication." (Psalm 130:1)
◆ "In whatever condition you were called, brothers and sisters, there remain with God." (1 Cor. 7:24)
◆ "And Jesus said to them, 'Follow me and I will make you fish for people.'" (Mark 1:17)

### Key words, ideas, and concepts to explore

◆ calling of the disciples;
◆ our calling into discipleship (at baptism);
◆ salvation;
◆ repentance.

### Stories to tell

◆ The stories of Jesus calling his disciples continue from Epiphany 2.

### Christian practice and liturgical tradition

See Epiphany 2, Year B above.

*Formation in baptismal discipleship*
See Epiphany 2, Year B above.


## The Fourth Sunday after the Epiphany, Year B
Lections: Deuteronomy 18:15-20; Psalm 111; 1 Corinthians 8:1b-13; Mark 1:21-28

### Theme of the lections
God's word, spoken and embodied in Jesus, is power.
  • *Epistle:* Instructions to the church at Corinth: Do not use your freedom in the gospel to tempt others to sin who are not so strong in their faith. Act always in love.

### Phrases for highlighting and memorization
  • "I will raise up for them a prophet like you from among their own people; I will put my words in the mouth of the prophet, who shall speak to them everything that I command." (Deut. 18:18)
  • "Great are the deeds of the LORD! they are studied by all who delight in them." (Psalm 111:2)
  • "But take care that this liberty of yours does not somehow become a stumbling block to the weak." (1 Cor. 8:9)
  • "They were all amazed, and they kept on asking one another, 'What is this? A new teaching—with authority! He commands even the unclean spirits, and they obey him.'" (Mark 1:27)

### Key words, ideas, and concepts to explore
  • prophets;
  • idols and false gods;
  • scribes;
  • unclean spirits;
  • exorcism;
  • tempting others to sin;
  • defeating the power of evil.

### Christian practice and liturgical tradition
  • Jesus had the power to drive out evil from the lives of people. Eucharistic Prayer B states, "In him, you have delivered us from evil, and made us worthy to stand before you"—a vivid reminder that Christ's presence in the eucharist stands between us and evil today.

- In the Lord's Prayer we ask to be delivered from evil.
- The Baptismal Covenant calls for the faithful to "persevere in resisting evil" (BCP 304).

### Formation in baptismal discipleship

The Christian is called to confront personal and societal evil as a part of the Baptismal Covenant: "Will you persevere in resisting evil, and, whenever you fall into sin, repent and return to the Lord?" (BCP 304).

## The Fifth Sunday after the Epiphany, Year B

Lections: 2 Kings 4:(8-17) 18-21 (22-31) 32-37; Psalm 142; 1 Corinthians 9:16-23; Mark 1:29-39

### Theme of the lections

God's power to heal is revealed in the life of the prophets and, above all, in the ministry of Jesus.

- *Epistle:* Paul enters into the life experience of each person he seeks to convert to the gospel.

### Phrases for highlighting and memorization

- "While [Elisha] lay bent over him, the flesh of the child became warm." (2 Kings 4:34b)
- "I cry to the LORD with my voice; to the LORD I make loud supplication." (Psalm 142:1)
- "I have become all things to all people, that I might by all means save some." (1 Cor. 9:22b)
- "[Jesus] came and took her by the hand and lifted her up. Then the fever left her, and she began to serve them." (Mark 1:31)

### Key words, ideas, and concepts to explore

- Elijah and Elisha, the great eighth-century prophets;
- the power of God to heal and restore life.

### Stories to tell

- The healing stories from 2 Kings and Mark.

### Christian practice and liturgical tradition

- We pray for healing in the Ministration to the Sick (BCP 453-461).

- In the Prayers of the People we pray for those in need of any kind of healing (BCP 383-393).

### Formation in baptismal discipleship
Congregations are called by their baptism into Christ, who heals and restores to life, to the ministry of healing. Intercessions at the eucharist are embodied by the baptized as they care for one another and as they witness to Christ's healing among them.

## The Sixth Sunday after the Epiphany, Year B
Lections: 2 Kings 5:1-15b; Psalm 42:1-7; 1 Corinthians 9:24-27; Mark 1:40-45

### Theme of the lections
God's promise of wholeness is revealed in acts of healing.
- *Epistle:* Running the race for an imperishable crown.

### Phrases for highlighting and memorization
- "If the prophet had commanded you to do something difficult, would you not have done it? How much more, when all he said to you was, 'Wash, and be clean'?" (2 Kings 5:13)
- "Put your trust in God; for I will yet give thanks to him, who is the help of my countenance, and my God." (Psalm 42:7)
- "Athletes exercise self-control in all things; they do it to receive a perishable wreath, but we an imperishable one." (1 Cor. 9:25)
- "But he went out and began to proclaim it freely, and to spread the word, so that Jesus could no longer go into a town openly, but stayed out in the country; and people came to him from every quarter." (Mark 1:45)

### Key words, ideas, and concepts to explore
- healing as a sign of God's power;
- Elisha the prophet;
- self-control.

### Stories to tell
- The story of Naaman from 2 Kings;
- The story of Jesus cleansing a leper from Mark.

*Christian practice and liturgical tradition*
See Epiphany 5, Year B above.

*Formation in baptismal discipleship*
See Epiphany 5, Year B above.


## The Seventh Sunday after the Epiphany, Year B
Lections: Isaiah 43:18-25; Psalm 32:1-8; 2 Corinthians 1:18-22; Mark 2:1-12

*Theme of the lections*
The power of God's forgiveness.
- *Epistle:* Paul's authority as an apostle comes straight from Jesus.

*Phrases for highlighting and memorization*
- "I am about to do a new thing; now it springs forth, do you not perceive it? I will make a way in the wilderness and rivers in the desert." (Isa. 43:19)
- "Happy are they whose transgressions are forgiven, and whose sin is put away." (Psalm 32:1)
- "For in him every one of God's promises is a 'Yes.'" (2 Cor. 1:20a)
- "'But so that you may know that the Son of Man has authority on earth to forgive sins'—[Jesus] said to the paralytic—'I say to you, stand up, take your mat and go to your home.'" (Mark 2:10-11)

*Key words, ideas, and concepts to explore*
- God's promise;
- healing;
- authority;
- forgiveness.

*Stories to tell*
- The gospel story of the healing of the paralytic.

*Christian practice and liturgical tradition*
- The formal prayers of the church are always offered "through Jesus Christ," reflecting the epistle text.

*Formation in baptismal discipleship*
The church is called to be a healing community.

## The Eighth Sunday after the Epiphany, Year B

Lections: Hosea 12:14-23; Psalm 103:1-6; 2 Corinthians 3:(4-11) 17–4:2; Mark 2:18-22

### Theme of the lections

Marriage as a metaphor describing the relationship between God and the faithful.

- *Epistle:* God's power and presence is evident in the life of Paul and the church.

### Phrases for highlighting and memorization

- "I will take you for my wife in faithfulness; and you shall know the LORD." (Hosea 2:20)
- "He satisfies you with good things, and your youth is renewed like an eagle's." (Psalm 103:5)
- "And all of us, with unveiled faces, seeing the glory of the Lord as though reflected in a mirror, are being transformed into the same image from one degree of glory to another; for this comes from the Lord, the Spirit." (2 Cor. 3:18)
- "Jesus said to them, 'The wedding guests cannot fast while the bridegroom is with them, can they? As long as they have the bridegroom with them, they cannot fast.'" (Mark 2:19)

### Key words, ideas, and concepts to explore

- glory;
- "unveiled faces";
- marriage customs in biblical times that shed light on today's lessons;
- the use of wineskins;
- fasting as a discipline;
- marriage as a symbol for the Body of Christ.

### Christian practice and liturgical tradition

- The "Exhortation" in the marriage rite (BCP 423) expresses the meaning behind today's lessons.

### Formation in baptismal discipleship

If the congregation is to reflect the gospel, then it will function more like a family than as an institution. To come into the church at baptism is to enter into a marriage-like relationship between the baptized and Christ as present in the church. Marriage, in turn, becomes a metaphor to understand Christian relationships between all people who reveal Christ's love for each other.


## The Last Sunday after the Epiphany, Year B

Lections: 1 Kings 19:9-18; Psalm 27:5-11; 2 Peter 1:16-19 (20-21); Mark 9:2-9

### Theme of the lections

The Transfiguration of our Lord.

- *Epistle:* Peter's account of the transfiguration.

### Phrases for highlighting and memorization

- "When Elijah heard it, he wrapped his face in his mantle and went out and stood at the entrance of the cave. Then there came a voice to him that said, 'What are you doing here, Elijah?'" (1 Kings 19:13)
- "For in the day of trouble he shall keep me safe in his shelter; he shall hide me in the secrecy of his dwelling and set me high upon a rock." (Psalm 27:7)
- "We ourselves heard this voice come from heaven, while we were with him on the holy mountain." (2 Peter 1:18)
- "And [Jesus] was transfigured before them, and his clothes became dazzling white, such as no one on earth could bleach them." (Mark 9:2b-3)

### Key words, ideas, and concepts to explore

- transfiguration;
- Moses and Elijah;
- holy mountain.

### Stories to tell

- The story of God and Elijah in 1 Kings;
- The story of Jesus' transfiguration.

### Christian practice and liturgical tradition

- The Sundays after the Epiphany are framed by both the Feast of the Epiphany, with its star in the heavens, and Jesus' face shining like the sun at the Transfiguration. The light of God's revelation in Jesus becomes clearer in the ensuing weeks as disciples are called and the word is proclaimed.

### Formation in baptismal discipleship

Each Sunday Christians gather "on the mountain top" in the assembly for the revelation of God so that we can see more clearly the way of Christ in our lives.

## ◆  ◆  Year C  ◆  ◆

## The Second Sunday after the Epiphany, Year C

Lections: Isaiah 62:1-5; Psalm 96:1-10; 1 Corinthians 12:1-11; John 2:1-11

### Theme of the lections

To be baptized is to have new life and to know the risen Christ.

- *Epistle:* All are empowered through baptism with spiritual gifts. (This Sunday begins a serialized reading of 1 Corinthians beginning at the twelfth chapter; therefore, the epistle reading will not usually be in thematic harmony with the Old Testament, psalm, and gospel lections.)

### Phrases for highlighting and memorization

- "For the LORD delights in you, and your land shall be married." (Isa. 62:4c)
- "Worship the Lord in the beauty of holiness; let the whole earth tremble before him." (Psalm 96:9)
- "Now there are varieties of gifts, but the same Spirit." (1 Cor. 12:4)
- "Jesus did this, the first of his signs, in Cana of Galilee, and revealed his glory; and his disciples believed him." (John 2:11)

### Key words, ideas, and concepts to explore

- the significance of names;
- spiritual gifts;

- "Jesus is Lord," the first creed of the church;
- wedding customs in biblical times;
- marriage as a metaphor of relationship with God;
- overview of 1 Corinthians.

### Stories to tell
- The wedding at Cana.

### Christian practice and liturgical tradition
- The wedding of Cana is mentioned in the opening exhortation of the Celebration and Blessing of a Marriage (BCP 423).

### Formation in baptismal discipleship
Baptism is not membership in the church. It is a calling into intimate relationship with God that can be expressed through the images of marriage, adoption, and birth into a family. The church emphasizes the ministry of the baptized, recognizing that everyone has been empowered by the Holy Spirit with spiritual gifts.

## The Third Sunday after the Epiphany, Year C
Lections: Nehemiah 8:2-10; Psalm 113; 1 Corinthians 12:12-27; Luke 4:12-21

### Theme of the lections
Scripture is to be heard, interpreted and embodied in the lives of God's people.
- *Epistle:* The church as the living Body of Christ.

### Phrases for highlighting and memorization
- "[The Levites] gave the sense, so that the people understood the reading." (Neh. 8:8b)
- "From the rising of the sun to its going down let the Name of the LORD be praised." (Psalm 113:3)
- "Now you are the body of Christ and individually members of it." (1 Cor. 12:27)
- "Then he began to say to them, 'Today this scripture has been fulfilled in your hearing.'" (Luke 4:21)

### Key words, ideas, and concepts to share
- the book of the law (Torah);
- the role of priests and Levites in biblical times;
- the Body of Christ;
- the synagogue in Jewish life;
- the power of the Spirit.

### Stories to tell
- The story of Ezra gathering the people together to hear the reading of the Torah. These were people who had lived in Babylonian exile and who needed to hear the story again in order to renew their identity as God's people.
- The story of Jesus reading and interpreting the words of Isaiah.

### Christian practice and liturgical tradition
- The ritual of reading the gospel at the eucharist comes out of the ancient rite described in today's first reading. Notice that the role of the Levite is to help the people understand the law. This describes the role of preacher and teacher in the church today.

### Formation in baptismal discipleship
As Jesus embodied the scripture in his life ("Today this scripture has been fulfilled in your hearing"), so the church is to embody God's word in the life of the congregation and each individual Christian.


## The Fourth Sunday after the Epiphany, Year C
Lections: Jeremiah 1:4-10; Psalm 71:1-6, 15-17; 1 Corinthians 14:12b-20; Luke 4:21-32

### Theme of the lections
To speak God's word is to risk rejection from those around us.
- *Epistle:* Instructions to those who have the gift of speaking in tongues.

### Phrases for highlighting and memorization
- "Now I have put my words in your mouth. See, today I appoint you over nations and over kingdoms, to pluck up and to pull down, to destroy and to overthrow, to build and to plant." (Jer. 1:9b-10)
- "O God, you have taught me since I was young, and to this day I tell of your wonderful works." (Psalm 71:17)

- "Since you are eager for spiritual gifts, strive to excel in them for building up the church." (1 Cor. 14:12b)
- "And [Jesus] said, 'Truly I tell you, no prophet is accepted in the prophet's hometown.'" (Luke 4:24)

### Key words, ideas, and concepts to explore
- the role of prophets;
- spiritual gifts;
- the gift of speaking in tongues.

### Stories to tell
- The story of Jesus' visit to Nazareth in Luke 4:14-30, pointing out the striking contrast between the way the people first receive Jesus and then their anger at him;
- The stories that lie behind Jesus' references in the gospel reading: the widow of Zarephath (1 Kings 17:8-24); the healing of Naaman the Syrian (2 Kings 5:1-19).

### Christian practice and liturgical tradition
- As Jesus proclaimed the word of God from Isaiah, he confronted the sinful pride of his own people. In the eucharistic liturgy, confession follows the hearing of the word. God's word confronts us, which leads to our acknowledgment of the gap between God's call and our response.

### Formation in baptismal discipleship
The readings for today confront the terrible cost of discipleship. To speak and act in God's name sets one apart.


## The Fifth Sunday after the Epiphany, Year C
Lections: Judges 6:11-24a; Psalm 85:7-13; 1 Corinthians 15:1-11; Luke 5:1-11

### Theme of the lections
The calling of the disciples to mission.
- *Epistle:* The resurrection lies at the heart of the proclamation of the gospel.

*Phrases for highlighting and memorization*
- "Then the LORD turned to [Gideon] and said, 'Go in this might of yours and deliver Israel from the hand of Midian; I hereby commission you.'" (Judges 6:14)
- "I will listen to what the LORD God is saying, for he is speaking peace to his faithful people and to those who turn their hearts to him." (Psalm 85:8)
- "For I handed on to you as of first importance what I in turn had received; that Christ died for our sins in accordance with the scriptures." (1 Cor. 15:3)
- "Then Jesus said to Simon, 'Do not be afraid; from now on you will be catching people.'" (Luke 5:10b)

*Key words, ideas, and concepts to explore*
- the gospel;
- resurrection appearances;
- the Midianites as enemies of Israel;
- God's call to Gideon, to the disciples, and to the church today.

*Stories to tell*
- Gideon's call;
- The calling of Peter, James, and John.

*Christian practice and liturgical tradition*
- The baptismal rite enacts the calling narratives heard in this week's readings. God calls disciples into baptism. Each Christian responds and turns to accept Jesus and reject evil. We hear God's word, accept the covenant, and receive the empowerment of the Holy Spirit for ministry in the world.

*Formation in baptismal discipleship*
At baptism every Christian is called into ministry. Simon Peter's call is the call of every Christian: "Follow me."

# The Sixth Sunday after the Epiphany, Year C

Lections: Jeremiah 17:5-10; Psalm 1; 1 Corinthians 15:12-20; Luke 6:17-26

### Theme of the lections

The Sermon on the Plain: God's way demands that the Christian makes choices that often put the faithful in conflict with those around them. (Note that a reading of Luke's equivalent to Matthew's Sermon on the Mount begins this Sunday.)

- *Epistle:* The resurrection is an absolutely essential element of the gospel of Jesus Christ.

### Phrases for highlighting and memorization

- "Blessed are those who trust in the LORD, whose trust is the LORD." (Jer. 17:7)
- "For the LORD knows the way of the righteous, but the way of the wicked is doomed." (Psalm 1:6)
- "If there is no resurrection of the dead, then Christ has not been raised; and if Christ has not been raised, then our proclamation has been in vain and your faith has been in vain." (1 Cor. 15:13)
- "Then [Jesus] looked up at his disciples and said: 'Blessed are you who are poor, for yours is the kingdom of God.'" (Luke 6:20)

### Key words, ideas, and concepts to explore

- the way of the righteous and the way of the wicked;
- proverbial sayings;
- resurrection;
- "first fruits";
- the Sermon on the Plain;
- blessedness;
- judgment results in a reversal of fortune.

### Christian practice and liturgical tradition

- The "Song of Mary" sung or said at Evening Prayer speaks of God bringing down the powerful and lifting up the lowly.

### Formation in baptismal discipleship

God's word is radical, and calls for a radical response. The words that Jesus spoke turned the world upside down for those who accepted them as God's word for them. The poor receive a kingdom. The hungry are satisfied. The life of the baptized must be formed in words and actions that "turn the world upside down" for the gospel of Jesus Christ. (See Isaiah 55:8-9: "For my thoughts are not your thoughts, nor are your ways my ways, says the LORD.")

## The Seventh Sunday after the Epiphany, Year C

Lections: Genesis 45:3-11, 21-28; Psalm 37:3-10; 1 Corinthians 15:35-38, 42-50; Luke 6:27-38

### Theme of the lections

The Sermon on the Plain: God's mercy must be expressed in the life of the Christian.

 ◆ *Epistle:* The resurrection is at the heart of Christian faith.

### Phrases for highlighting and memorization

 ◆ "[Joseph] said, 'I am your brother, Joseph, whom you sold into Egypt. And now do not be distressed, or angry with yourselves, because you sold me here; for God sent me before you to preserve life.'" (Gen. 45:4b-5)
 ◆ "Put your trust in the LORD and do good; dwell in the land and feed on its riches." (Psalm 37:3)
 ◆ "What you sow does not come to life unless it dies." (1 Cor. 15:36)
 ◆ "Be merciful, just as your Father is merciful." (Luke 6:36)

### Key words, ideas, and concepts to explore

 ◆ God's mercy;
 ◆ forgiveness;
 ◆ resurrection;
 ◆ the Sermon on the Plain;
 ◆ the ethics of Jesus.

### Stories to tell

 ◆ The story of Joseph forgiving his brothers from Genesis.

### Christian practice and liturgical tradition

 ◆ The passing of the peace expresses a forgiving community at worship.
 ◆ The resurrection is at the heart of Christian teaching, prayer, and creed.

### Formation in baptismal discipleship

The Christian congregation aspires to live the higher standards of the gospel. Enmity and harsh judgments have no place in the assembly.

## The Eight Sunday after the Epiphany, Year C

Lections: Jeremiah 7:1-7 (8-15); Psalm 92:1-5, 11-14; 1 Corinthians 15:50-58; Luke 6:39-49

### Theme of the lections

The Sermon on the Plain: Our actions must match our words in response to God's covenant.

- ◆ *Epistle:* God's power revealed in Jesus destroys even death.

### Phrases for highlighting and memorization

- ◆ "For if you truly amend your ways and your doings, if you truly act justly one with another, if you do not oppress the alien, the orphan, and the widow, or shed innocent blood in this place, and if you do not go after other gods to your own hurt, then I will dwell with you in this place, in the land that I gave of old to your ancestors forever and ever." (Jer. 7:5-7)
- ◆ "The righteous shall flourish like a palm tree, and shall spread abroad like a cedar of Lebanon." (Psalm 92:11)
- ◆ "And as for what you sow, you do not sow the body that is to be, but a bare seed, perhaps of wheat or of some other grain." (1 Cor. 15:37)
- ◆ "That one is like a man building a house, who dug deeply and laid the foundation on rock; when a flood arose, the river burst against that house but could not shake it, because it had been well built." (Luke 6:48)

### Key words, ideas, and concepts to explore

- ◆ the Sermon on the Plain;
- ◆ resurrection;
- ◆ sowing seed;
- ◆ building on a foundation;
- ◆ God's victory revealed in Jesus.

### Stories to tell
- The gospel story of the man building a house.

### Christian practice and liturgical tradition
- The centrality of self-examination and confession in the life of the church is expressed in Prayer Book worship. The Litany of Penitence for Ash Wednesday (BCP 267-269) offers a striking illustration of today's lessons.
- Prayers for those who have died are a constant reminder that these relationships go on beyond the grave.

### Formation in baptismal discipleship
The Baptismal Covenant stresses continuing in "the apostles' teaching and fellowship" (BCP 304). The centrality of living in a community centered on God's word lies at the heart of Christian formation.

## The Last Sunday after the Epiphany, Year C
Lections: Exodus 34:29-35; Psalm 99; 1 Corinthians 12:27–13:13; Luke 9:28-36

### Theme of the lections
The Transfiguration of our Lord.
- *Epistle:* Recognizing the diverse gifts of the Holy Spirit. All are one in the Body of Christ.

### Phrases for highlighting and memorization
- "Moses did not know that the skin of his face shone because he had been talking with God." (Exod. 34:29b)
- "Proclaim the greatness of the LORD our God and worship him upon his holy hill; for the LORD our God is the Holy One." (Psalm 99:9)
- "Now you are the body of Christ and individually members of it." (1 Cor. 12:27)
- "Then from the cloud came a voice that said, 'This is my Son, my Chosen; listen to him!'" (Luke 9:35)

### Key words, ideas, and concepts to explore
- transfiguration;
- Body of Christ;
- gifts of the Spirit.

### Stories to tell

- The story of Jesus' transfiguration;
- The story of Moses speaking with God.

### Christian practice and liturgical tradition

- The Sundays after the Epiphany are framed by both the Feast of the Epiphany, with its star in the heavens, and Jesus' face shining like the sun at the Transfiguration. The light of God's revelation in Jesus becomes clearer in the ensuing weeks as disciples are called and the word is proclaimed.

### Formation in baptismal discipleship

The ministry of the baptized is expressed in the epistle lesson. All who have been baptized are an integral part of the Body of Christ. All have gifts that are essential for the Body to function effectively. No one gift is greater than another.

# *Lent*

## Definition

"Lent" comes from the Anglo-Saxon word *lencton*—the time of year when the days grow long. The season begins on Ash Wednesday and ends with the Easter Triduum that includes Maundy Thursday through Easter Sunday, covering forty days (excluding Sundays). Since every Sunday is a "little Easter" celebrating the Resurrection, Sundays remain feast days even during the solemn Lenten season. The five Lenten Sundays are followed by the Sunday of the Passion (Palm Sunday), which ushers in Holy Week.

In the early church, Lent was the time of preparation for the Easter baptism of converts to the faith. Persons who were to receive the sacrament of baptism—"new birth," "death to sin"—were expected to fast and prepare during these weeks. As noted below, the Bible readings appointed for the five Sundays in Lent provide a short course in the meaning of baptism.

## Holy Days in Lent

Because Lent is determined by the movable date of Easter Day, it is necessary to check the Calendar of the Church Year (BCP 15-33) for the holy days, lesser feasts, or other special observances that occur during Lent in a particular year.

## Lenten Themes

◆ Baptism—The major theme of the season is the meaning of baptism, which reflects the origins and continuing focus of the season. Lent is a time of preparation for baptism at the Easter Vigil; in the early church, this was the only time baptisms occurred. Candidates for baptism were led through the stories of the Bible that helped them examine the nature of the life they were about to enter. Through the experience of fasting, self-denial, and acknowledgment of their need to repent and turn to God, they began to live out Paul's vision of offering oneself to God:

> *I appeal to you therefore, brothers and sisters, by the mercies of God, to present your bodies as a living sacrifice, holy and acceptable to God, which is your spiritual worship.* (Rom. 12:1)

- Fasting—The forty weekdays of Lent represent the days of fasting and temptation that Jesus spent in the wilderness. Self-denial is an opportunity for discipline, the sacrifice of our will to the purpose of God.
- Reconciliation—Lent is a time for reconciliation with God, self, and others.
- Discipleship—During the Lenten season we consider the nature of the ministry of Jesus and what it means to be a disciple.

## Great Words of Lent

| | |
|---|---|
| Atonement | Overcoming temptation |
| Calvary | Penitence |
| Catechesis (teaching the faith) | Pilgrimage |
| Catechumenate | Preparation |
| Catechumens | Redemption |
| Contrition | Return to God |
| Conversion | Sacrifice |
| Cross | Salvation |
| Crucifix | Self-denial |
| Fasting | Social justice |
| Humility | Reconciliation |
| Meditation | Wilderness |

## Lent Through the Eyes of a Child

Lent is:

- a time for looking at the things we have done that are wrong, asking God's and other people's forgiveness;
- a time for giving up the things that keep us from being loving people;
- a time for doing extra things that will help us grow closer to God;
- a time to be more aware of what it means to love as God loves us;

- a time to ask God to help us to be more loving, remembering that God is always ready to strengthen us.
- a time to think about our baptism and what it means to be a child of God.

## Symbols and Traditions of Lent

- Color—purple, for penitence and royalty, or rough linen or a similar material, unbleached, raw, plain, and austere, to reflect the mood of Lent (based upon the sackcloth of Old Testament mourning).
- Ashes—prepared from the previous year's palms for Ash Wednesday to symbolize our mortality and sorrow for our sins. The people of the Hebrew scriptures put ashes on their foreheads as a sign of penitence. Job (Job 42:6) and the king of Nineveh (Jonah 3:6) repented in ashes, wearing sackcloth.
- Alleluias, joyful canticles, the *Gloria in excelsis*—omitted from worship and replaced with songs and responses that are more in keeping with Lent's contemplative mood.
- Vestments and hangings—more austere and solemn; flowers may be omitted from the altar.
- Shrove Tuesday—the day before Lent begins on Ash Wednesday. On this day it used to be the custom to use up all milk, eggs, and fat in a household since these were not allowed in the strict fasting of Lent. The ingredients were made into pancakes, a meal which came to symbolize preparation for the discipline of Lent. "Shrove" comes from the verb "to shrive" (to confess and receive absolution), referring to the ancient practice of confessing sins and receiving absolution in order to begin and keep a holy Lent. Other names for this day include *Carnival*, meaning "farewell to meat," and *Mardi Gras*, meaning "Fat Tuesday." Some congregations offer a carnival-type event as a part of their Shrove Tuesday preparation for Lent.
- The cross—symbol of Christ and his sacrifice, love, salvation, redemption, atonement, and victory.
- Retreat time—during Lent time is set aside for teaching and learning, spiritual growth, fasting and self-denial, meditation and retreats.
- Conversion and repentance—as a preparation for baptism or the renewal of baptismal vows at Easter.
- Stations of the Cross—began in the Holy Land as a series of devotions along the *Via Dolorosa* (Way of Sorrow) and later spread to parish

churches, where the faithful stop to pray and reflect along a way that outlines Jesus' passion.

- Preparation for baptism—historically a period to prepare for the baptisms and confirmations that traditionally occur at the Vigil of Easter.

## Social Justice Themes for Lent

*Ash Wednesday*

Ethical issues are raised in the Litany of Penitence (BCP 267-269):
- exploitation of other people;
- dishonesty in daily life and work;
- indifference to injustice, human need, suffering, and cruelty;
- prejudice and contempt toward those who differ from us;
- waste and pollution of God's creation.

As we explore more fully the Baptismal Covenant and the covenant of the Torah, we become increasingly aware of how far we have strayed from God's ways.

*The Second Sunday in Lent*

God's mercy for us calls for mercy from us:
- criminal justice issues;
- death penalty;
- treatment of refugees and displaced persons.

## Great Bible Stories for Lent

See the stories listed in connection with the propers appointed for each Sunday in Lent.

## Great Hymns of Lent

Lenten hymns 140 to 152, including:
- Forty days and forty nights (Hymn 150);
- The glory of these forty days (Hymn 143).

### Services with Lenten Themes

- The Daily Office (BCP 37-135) reflects the discipline of prayer and the regular reading of the Bible;
- Reconciliation of a Penitent (BCP 447-452);
- A Penitential Order (BCP 319-321/351-353);
- The Great Litany (BCP 148-155).

## Living the Lenten Season at Home and in the Parish

- Write and illustrate Litanies of Penitence by children and/or adults.
- Dramatize the gospel lessons and other readings that are especially rich in Lent and lend themselves to participation by a large group. Think about using taped "radio plays" or sound effects, or about using slides, pantomime, puppets, or shadow plays, as well as choral readings and dramatic presentations.
- A study or review of our faith as Episcopalians might focus upon An Outline of the Faith (BCP 845-862).
- "Bury the Alleluia" is a medieval Christian tradition. Make an "Alleluia" as a painting, small banner, plaque (possibilities are numerous). Wrap it in plastic or cloth to protect it, put it in a box, and bury it on the last Sunday *before* Lent. On Easter Day dig it up and display it, singing, "Jesus Christ is risen today! Alleluia!"
- Jesus the True Bread is part of the collect of Lent's fourth Sunday. Sponsor a day for family breadbaking, or a day of baking bread for a eucharist (perhaps for Easter Day). Fancy breads can be frozen for an Easter feast.
- A Lenten pilgrimage can offer opportunities for reading and reflection done either all at one time or for a shorter time each week. It can be done at home or at designated quiet areas in the church building. Instructions may include bringing a Bible, paper, and pencil; a simple guide sheet will help the "pilgrims" begin. Brief suggested readings might be the epistles or other readings for Lent, one for each "station," with a short commentary and questions to aid in reflection. "Pilgrims" move at their own pace, using the guide sheet to meet their own schedule and needs. Perhaps the last "station" will be the altar rail, reading an account of the Easter story or some other passage that points toward the climax for which Lent is a preparation.

- Remembering our heritage, some selections that might be memorized are:
  - —The Lord's Prayer (BCP 97);
  - —The Apostles' Creed (BCP 96);
  - —The Ten Commandments (BCP 350);
  - —The names of the books of the Bible;
  - —The Twenty-third Psalm (BCP 612-613);
  - —A Table Blessing (BCP 835);
  - —A Collect for the Renewal of Life (BCP 99);
  - —Antiphon of the Song of Simeon (BCP 134): "Guide us waking, O Lord...";
  - —A prayer: "Keep watch, dear Lord, with those who work..." (BCP 134).

# The Sundays in Lent

## An Overview of the Readings

During Lent the readings of the five weeks of the season provide us with a short course in the meaning of baptism. This is no accident, of course. When the early church prepared candidates for baptism, it let the liturgy do the teaching. Some of the Lenten texts found in the lectionary of our Prayer Book were teaching texts for candidates for baptism in the early centuries of Christianity.

With that thought in mind, the outline below for the Sundays in Lent differs from the treatment of Sunday lections for the rest of the year. The focus of the lections each week has a direct reference to parts of the baptismal rite in *The Book of Common Prayer*. Following the theme of the lectionary texts week by week, the congregation will have an opportunity to explore the baptismal rite in Year A and Year B. In Year C, five great themes of baptism are explored during Lent.

If Lent provides a natural way of discovering the meaning of baptism, there is no need to wonder what we should be doing for a Lenten program! The lectionary provides the "program," one that developed out of the early church's preparation of candidates for their baptism at the Easter Vigil.

The church's renewed interest in the catechumenal process today makes baptismal teaching even more relevant to the congregations of the church.

Notice the close connection among all three readings in the five weeks of Lent. Unlike the epistle lections in the Sundays after the Epiphany and after Pentecost, when entire epistles are read independently of the gospel, the epistle lections during Lent are linked directly with the baptismal theme expressed in the other two readings.

Since baptism and Lent are all about conversion, the themes for these five weeks also provide us with a process for "conversion therapy" (a term used by Aidan Kavanagh to describe the purpose behind the catechumenate) as we move through the season and Holy Week. First we turn away from evil and toward Jesus Christ (Lent 1 and 2). Then we look at what we thirst for in life and ask for the empowerment of the Holy Spirit (Lent 3 and 4). Then we put our whole life and trust in Christ, who leads us even through death into life (Lent 5).

## ❖ ❖ Year A ❖ ❖

## The First Sunday in Lent, Year A

### The baptismal rite
The renunciations:

> Do you renounce Satan and all the spiritual forces of wickedness that rebel against God? Do you renounce the evil powers of this world which corrupt and destroy the creatures of God? Do you renounce all sinful desires that draw you from the love of God? (BCP 302)

### Baptismal theme expressed in the lectionary readings
Saying "no" to evil so that the Christian can say "yes" to Christ.

### The lectionary readings
*Hebrew scriptures: Genesis 2:4b-9, 15-17, 25–3:7*

> The story of Adam and Eve, who said "yes" when they were called by God to say "no."

*Epistle: Romans 5:12-19 (20-21)*

A comparison between Adam and Christ.

♦ During Lent in Year A, the readings provide a primer in Christianity as outlined in Paul's letters to the Romans and Ephesians. These epistle readings pick up the theme from the Hebrew scripture readings and the gospel.

*Gospel: Matthew 4:1-11*

Jesus' temptation in the wilderness. The response to the devil is "no."

## The Second Sunday in Lent, Year A

### The baptismal rite

Turning and accepting Jesus as Savior and Lord:

*Do you turn to Jesus Christ and accept him as your Savior? Do you put your whole trust in his grace and love? Do you promise to follow and obey him as your Lord?* (BCP 302-303)

### Baptismal theme expressed in the lectionary readings

Saying "yes" to Jesus.

### The lectionary readings

*Hebrew scriptures: Genesis 12:1-8*

God calls Abraham and Sarah to leave their country and people and go to the land of Canaan.

*Epistle: Romans 4:1-5 (6-12) 13-17*

Abraham is justified by faith.

*Gospel: John 3:1-17*

The need for the rebirth of baptism. The story of Nicodemus. "Very truly, I tell you, no one can enter the kingdom of God without being born of water and Spirit."

## The Third Sunday in Lent, Year A

### *The baptismal rite*
The waters of baptism:

> *Now sanctify this water, we pray you, by the power of your Holy Spirit, that those who here are cleansed from sin and born again may continue for ever in the risen life of Jesus Christ our Savior.* (BCP 307)

### *Baptismal theme expressed in the lectionary readings*
The baptismal waters become for the Christian "a spring of water gushing up to eternal life" (John 4:14).

### *The lectionary readings*
*Hebrew scriptures: Exodus 17:1-7*
> God leads the thirsty Israelites to water from the rock at Meribah.

*Epistle: Romans 5:1-11*
> Faith leads to salvation.

*Gospel: John 4:5-26 (27-38) 39-42*
> The Samaritan woman who comes to the well for water finds her thirst assuaged by Jesus, who promises her living water.

## The Fourth Sunday in Lent, Year A

### *The baptismal rite*
The anointing of baptism:

> *N., you are sealed by the Holy Spirit in Baptism and marked as Christ's own for ever.* (BCP 308)

### *Baptismal theme expressed in the lectionary readings*
The Christian is given the gift of enlightenment through the Holy Spirit.

### *The lectionary readings*
*Hebrew scriptures: 1 Samuel 16:1-13*
> As David was anointed by Samuel, he was empowered to speak for God as Israel's king.

*Epistle: Ephesians 5:(1-7) 8-14*
> Christians are called to "live as children of light."

*Gospel: John 9:1-13 (14-27) 28-38*

The story of the healing of the man born blind. Jesus spat on the ground and make a paste with his spittle with which he anointed the man's eyes. Through the anointing of Jesus the blind man could see to follow Jesus: "'Lord, I believe.' And he worshiped him" (John 9:38). Through the anointing of the Holy Spirit at baptism the Christian can see to follow Jesus. The early church saw the healing of the man born blind as a metaphor of enlightenment: the Christian is called to see things differently.

## The Fifth Sunday in Lent, Year A

### The baptismal rite

The forgiveness of sins and new life through baptism:

*Heavenly Father, we thank you that by water and the Holy Spirit you have bestowed upon these your servants the forgiveness of sin, and raised them to the new life of grace.* (BCP 308)

### Baptismal theme expressed in the lectionary readings

In baptism the Christian is freed from the tomb of sinfulness. Dry bones take on flesh and those who were dead are filled with the breath of God. The raising of Lazarus points ahead to the Resurrection.

### The lectionary readings

*Hebrew scriptures: Ezekiel 37:1-3 (4-10) 11-14*

In an intense vision, Ezekiel sees the dry bones of the house of Israel lying in a valley. As Ezekiel speaks God's words over the bones, they take on sinew and flesh and come alive in the breath of God.

*Epistle: Romans 6:16-23*

The Christian is freed from the slavery of sin. "For the wages of sin is death, but the free gift of God is eternal life in Christ Jesus our Lord."

*Gospel: John 11:(1-16) 17-44*

The raising of Lazarus.

# ◆ ◆ Year B ◆ ◆

## The First Sunday in Lent, Year B

### The baptismal rite

The need for conversion is expressed in the baptismal entrance rite as well as in the renunciations of evil:

> *There is one Body and one Spirit. There is one hope in God's call to us.*
> (BCP 299)
> *Do you renounce Satan and all the spiritual forces of wickedness that rebel against God?* (BCP 302)

### Baptismal theme expressed in the lectionary readings

- ◆ Noah and the ark: We must turn from evil and accept the covenant of salvation.
- ◆ Jesus' temptations: What tempts us away from our baptismal ministry?

### The lectionary readings

*Hebrew scriptures: Genesis 9:8-17*

The covenant with Noah.

*Epistle: 1 Peter 3:18-22*

The epistle reading refers to the story of the ark in Genesis, seeing it as a prefigurement of the salvation we receive through baptism. To be baptized is to enter into the ark and be "saved" from the swirling waters of death. Note that the word "nave," denoting the place where the congregation gathers, is related to Latin word for "ship" *(navy)*.

*Gospel: Mark 1:9-13*

The temptations of Jesus.

## The Second Sunday in Lent, Year B

### The baptismal rite

In our baptism we offer ourselves to God in Christ, for in the water of baptism "we are buried with Christ in his death" (BCP 306). This sacrifice of self is reinforced at every celebration of the eucharist, where we offer "our selves, our souls and bodies, to be a reasonable, holy, and living sacrifice" to God (BCP 336). Each eucharistic prayer makes some reference to self-offering.

### Baptismal theme expressed in the lectionary readings
Saying "yes" to Jesus Christ and offering our lives to God in Christ.

### The lectionary readings
*Hebrew scriptures: Genesis 22:1-14*
> The story of Abraham's call to sacrifice Isaac.

*Epistle: Romans 8:31-39*
> Paul's triumphant words of assurance that nothing can separate us from the love of God.

*Gospel: Mark 8:31-38*
> Jesus says that the Son of Man must undergo great suffering and his followers must take up their cross and follow him:
> > *If any want to become my followers, let them deny themselves and take up their cross and follow me. For those who want to save their life will lose it, and those who lose their life for my sake, and for the sake of the gospel, will save it.* (Mark 8:34b-35)

## The Third Sunday in Lent, Year B

### The baptismal rite
The Baptismal Covenant (BCP 304-305).

### Baptismal theme expressed in the lectionary readings
We are called into a covenant relationship with God at baptism. In Christ there is a *new* covenant symbolized by Jesus' action of cleansing the temple. In the new covenant, Jesus' body becomes the meeting place between God and creation, rather than the temple in Jerusalem. Paul reminds his readers that the former covenant does not bring life, but only frustration and anguish.

### The lectionary readings
*Hebrew scriptures: Exodus 20:1-17*
> The Ten Commandments can be viewed as a synopsis of the 613 commandments of the Torah. We are called into a relationship with God

in which we love the Lord above all others and our neighbors as ourselves.

*Epistle: Romans 7:13-25*

Paul shares his struggle. The harder he tries to follow the Law of the Covenant, the more he is confronted by the sinfulness in his own nature. His conclusion is that though the Law of the Covenant is essential, it is the saving act of Jesus that makes us righteous before God and not the hopeless struggle to find salvation through keeping the Law.

*Gospel: John 2:13-22*

Jesus enters the temple and cleanses it. He speaks of his own body becoming the new temple.

## The Fourth Sunday in Lent, Year B

### The baptismal rite

The Prayers for the Candidates:

*Deliver them, O Lord, from the way of sin and death. Open their hearts to your grace and truth. Fill them with your holy and life-giving Spirit. Keep them in the faith and communion of your holy Church. Teach them to love others in the power of the Spirit. Send them into the world in witness to your love. Bring them to the fullness of your peace and glory.*
(BCP 305)

### Baptismal theme expressed in the lectionary readings

God continues to call people back from exile. Salvation (salving/ healing) comes as a gift of grace. The eucharist is the proclamation that Christ sustains us on our journey back from exile. It points to the heavenly banquet where all the faithful will gather with those who have gone before to sing praises to God: "Holy, holy, holy Lord, God of power and might...."

### The lectionary readings

*Hebrew scriptures: 2 Chronicles 36:14-23*

The writer describes the Babylonian exile. The people of Judah were sent off to Babylonia for "seventy years" by the Babylonians and only restored when King Cyrus of Persia conquered the Babylonians and allowed the Jews to return to their homeland. The writer of the account reminds the reader that people went into exile because they were unfaithful to God.

*Epistle: Ephesians 2:4-10*

> A ringing proclamation that we have been saved through God's grace.

*Gospel: John 6:4-15*

> The account of the feeding of the five thousand points to the eucharist and the messianic banquet.

## The Fifth Sunday in Lent, Year B

### The baptismal rite

The Thanksgiving over the Water:

> *We thank you, Father, for the water of Baptism. In it we are buried with Christ in his death. By it we share in his resurrection.* (BCP 306)

This baptismal text comes straight from St. Paul:

> *Therefore we have been buried with (Christ) by baptism into death, so that, just as Christ was raised from the dead by the glory of the Father, so we too might walk in newness of life.* (Rom. 6:4)

The Easter Vigil is a liturgical enactment of that process of entering into Christ's death so that we may have life.

> *Almighty God, whose most dear Son went not up to joy but first he suffered pain, and entered not into glory before he was crucified: Mercifully grant that we, walking in the way of the cross, may find it none other than the way of life and peace; through Jesus Christ our Lord.* (BCP 272)

### Baptismal theme expressed in the lectionary readings

In Jesus' death and resurrection and through our baptism, we have a covenant with God written on our hearts.

### The lectionary readings

*Hebrew scriptures: Jeremiah 31:31-34*

> Jeremiah's ringing words of promise are shared. The day will come when God will make a new covenant with the people written on their hearts rather than on stone.

*Epistle: Hebrews 5:(1-4) 5-10*

> Christ is the eternal high priest who acts as the perfect mediator between God and all people.

*Gospel: John 12:20-33*

By losing his life, Jesus brings life for others. A follower of Jesus must look at death and life in the same way.

# ◆ ◆ Year C ◆ ◆

## The First Sunday in Lent, Year C

In Year C we begin an exploration of five great themes related to baptism.

### Baptismal theme: Creed

The Apostles' Creed, in which belief leads to faithfulness:

*I believe in God, the Father almighty, creator of heaven and earth....*
(BCP 304)

### Baptismal theme expressed in the lectionary readings

Belief and acceptance of Jesus as Lord. The ancient creed outlining God's mighty acts for Israel spoken at the time of offering the first fruits of the harvest is matched in this week's readings by the simple statement from Romans, "Jesus is Lord." Jesus responded to temptation by his own "creed" taken from Deuteronomy: "One does not live by bread alone...Worship the Lord your God, and serve only him...Do not put the Lord your God to the test."

### The lectionary readings

*Hebrew scriptures: Deuteronomy 26:(1-4) 5-11*

The text describes an ancient liturgical rite prescribed for the offering of the first fruits of the harvest. The statement forms a creed that is to be proclaimed by the faithful recounting what God has done for Israel.

*Epistle: Romans 10:(5-8a) 8b-13*

The second reading is a creed. "If you confess with your lips that Jesus is Lord and believe in your heart that God raised him from the dead, you will be saved." The three simple words "Jesus is Lord" are the church's earliest creed.

*Gospel: Luke 4:1-13*

Jesus' temptation in the wilderness following his baptism.

*Baptismal theme: Covenant*

The Baptismal Covenant:

> *Let us join with those who are committing themselves to Christ and renew our own baptismal covenant.* (BCP 303)

*Baptismal theme expressed in the lectionary readings*

The Baptismal Covenant in *The Book of Common Prayer* includes the Apostles' Creed followed by five statements of our commitment to live according to our beliefs. The response to each statement of commitment is the same: "I will, with God's help." Keeping covenant means making right choices (the narrow road), and joining Jesus "on the way" to Jerusalem.

*The lectionary readings*

*Hebrew scriptures: Genesis 15:1-12, 17-18*

> God establishes a covenant with Abraham. Abraham's faith is what made him righteous before God. The covenant-making rite described in this text indicates the serious nature of the relationship being established between Abraham and Sarah's descendants and God.

*Epistle: Philippians 3:17–4:1*

> Paul announces the true citizenship of the faithful in Philippi: they are citizens of heaven. That is, they live in the world with a different vision and set of values than the people around them. Their total commitment is to God's plan rather than to the momentary satisfaction of "the belly." Paul sets the example for Christian life. Jesus will "transform the body of our humiliation that it may be conformed to the body of his glory."

*Gospel: Luke 13:(22-30) 31-35*

> (Verses 22-30 heighten the point Jesus was making and are important to share with catechumens and those who are reaffirming their baptismal vows.) Jesus responds to the question of how many will be saved with strong words of warning: "Strive to enter through the narrow door." The householder will rise up and shut the door, and some who thought they were "in" will find they were "out." Others will come and "eat in the kingdom of God."

### Baptismal theme: Calling

The welcome given to the newly baptized:

> We receive you into the household of God. Confess the faith of Christ crucified, proclaim his resurrection, and share with us in his eternal priesthood. (BCP 308)

### Baptismal theme expressed in the lectionary readings

Baptism is a calling into ministry. For the Christian, baptism is the "burning bush" experience that makes sense of the rest of one's life in Christ. The fact that baptism comes for many at infancy means that the church must constantly look back to baptism to reaffirm the sacred calling to participate with God in continuing acts of salvation. The gospel reading is a solemn reminder that with the call comes accountability. God expects the Christian and the church to bear fruit: "If it bears fruit next year, well and good; but if not, you can cut it down" (Luke 13:9).

### The lectionary readings

*Hebrew scriptures: Exodus 3:1-15*

The call of Moses at the burning bush to lead the Israelites out from their slavery in Egypt.

*Epistle: 1 Corinthians 10:1-13*

The Exodus story is to be a lesson for all Christians, Paul wrote. Though all the Hebrew people passed through the Sea of Reeds, not all of them were faithful. We cannot take our baptism (our Sea of Reeds experience) for granted. Our response to the event of our baptism is the test of our righteousness before God.

*Gospel: Luke 13:1-9*

In the gospel reading Jesus stresses the need for repentance. We never know when a final accounting will be called for.

### Baptismal theme: Eucharist

The Holy Eucharist is the sacrament of baptismal renewal and reconciliation, and a foretaste of the Reign of God:

> *Offer to God a sacrifice of thanksgiving, and make good your vows to the Most High"* (offertory sentence at the eucharist, BCP 376).

### Baptismal theme expressed in the lectionary readings

"Holy Baptism is appropriately administered within the Eucharist as the chief service on a Sunday or other feast" (rubric, BCP 298). It has been said that the eucharist is the only "repeatable" part of the baptismal rite. Those made sons and daughters of God at their baptism are welcomed to the feast of the eucharist as the prodigal son was welcomed by his father with sandals, a ring, and feasting. Christians are fed for the journey both as a remembrance and as a promise.

### The lectionary readings

*Hebrew scriptures: Joshua (4:19-24) 5:9-12*

> Israel crossed the Jordan and at last entered the land of Canaan. Read Joshua 4:1–5:12 to see the context of the assigned reading on this fourth Sunday in Lent. The daily feeding of manna was replaced with the harvested crops available in the new land.

> The first Passover was celebrated as the Israelites prepared to leave Egypt a generation earlier. Now as the people pass through the Jordan River, Passover was celebrated again. Exodus 12:14 commands that it be celebrated "as a festival to the LORD; throughout your generations you shall observe it as a perpetual ordinance." In the reading for this fourth Sunday, there is a liturgical feeling to the scene described. A procession moves across the Jordan. Stones are erected as "a memorial." Bread is shared both as a remembrance and as a promise.

> The Jewish Passover lies at the heart of the Christian eucharist: "Christ our Passover is sacrificed for us" (BCP 364). Jesus is the manna for the Christian:

> *I am the bread of life. Your ancestors ate the manna in the wilderness, and they died....Whoever eats of this bread will live forever; and the*

*bread that I will give for the life of the world is my flesh. (John 6:48-49, 51b)*

*Epistle: 2 Corinthians 5:17-21*

Christians are a whole new creation and must see themselves as "ambassadors of Christ" in the world.

*So if anyone is in Christ, there is a new creation: everything old has passed away; see, everything has become new! All this is from God, who reconciled us to himself through Christ, and has given us the ministry of reconciliation. (2 Cor. 17-18)*

Baptism makes us that new creation. We are "born again." The ministry of reconciliation points ahead to the gospel reading and the eucharist.

*Gospel: Luke 15:11-32*

The parable of the prodigal son. As the younger son was welcomed by the father and invited to the banquet, so we are welcomed as daughters and sons and invited to the eucharist. At the passing of the peace we repeat the act of the father toward his son: "But while he was still far off, his father saw him and was filled with compassion; he ran and put his arms around him and kissed him" (Luke 15:20b). As the epistle reading so beautifully reminds us, this simple act of reconciliation is to be our ministry in the world as well.

## The Fifth Sunday in Lent, Year C

### Baptismal theme: Promise

The Thanksgiving over the Water:

*We thank you Father, for the water of Baptism. In it we are buried with Christ in his death. By it we share in his resurrection. Through it we are reborn by the Holy Spirit. Therefore in joyful obedience to your Son, we bring into his fellowship those who come to him in faith, baptizing them in the Name of the Father, and of the Son, and of the Holy Spirit. (BCP 306-307)*

### Baptismal theme expressed in the lectionary readings

God did a "new thing" as Moses led the slaves of Egypt through the water of the Sea of Reeds into the wilderness of Sinai. God did a "new thing" as Joshua led the people across the Jordan River and celebrated Passover in the promised land. God promises a "new thing," a "new Exodus" when water will flow in the desert for God's people. God does a "new thing" in leading Christians into the waters of baptism where they are "buried with Christ" so that they may "share in his resurrection."

### The lectionary readings
*Hebrew scriptures: Isaiah 43:16-21*

A new Exodus is promised to God's people living in Babylonian exile. This will be an even more marvelous Exodus than the first one: "I am about to do a new thing; now it springs forth, do you not perceive it? I will make a way in the wilderness and rivers in the desert" (Isa. 43:19).

*Epistle: Philippians 3:8-14*

There is nothing more important to Paul than his relationship with Christ. Everything that he considered important before his turning to Christ now means nothing. Paul wants to know Christ "and the power of his resurrection and the sharing of his sufferings by becoming like him in his death, if somehow I may attain the resurrection from the dead" (Phil. 3:10-11).

*Gospel: Luke 20:9-19*

Jesus tells the parable of the wicked tenants, a story of warning and promise. God's people are tenants, not owners, of the "vineyard" that is the Christian's life and ministry. Accountability and stewardship are the key to responding to the baptismal call in faith.

# *Holy Week*

## Definition

In Holy Week the church dramatizes the events leading up to and including the suffering and death of Jesus on the cross. Holy Week begins with the Sunday of the Passion, or Palm Sunday, and the joyous triumphal entry into Jerusalem, and ends with the Triduum (*Triduum Sacrum,* meaning in Latin "the sacred three days"), which begins with the celebration of the eucharist on Maundy Thursday and ends with the vespers of Easter Sunday evening.

The name Maundy Thursday comes from the Latin *mandatum* or "command," from the words attributed to Jesus in the gospel of John: "I give you a new commandment, that you love one another. Just as I have loved you, you also should love one another" (John 13:34). Good Friday commemorates the crucifixion of our Lord. It is known as "Good" because of the new life brought about by his victory of the cross.

## Holy Week Themes

The principal theme of Holy Week is Jesus' passion: "No one has greater love than this, to lay down one's life for one's friends" (John 15:13). Jesus gives his life to save us from sin and death.

The language of sacrifice is difficult to understand. The New Testament draws heavily on the sacrificial practices of the temple in describing the unique role of Jesus in bringing salvation through the cross. Paschal lambs were sacrificed at Passover, and Jesus' death on the cross was seen in the light of that temple practice. He is the true paschal lamb offered, finally, for the sins of the whole world. Without that background of temple practice, some of the language about Jesus' death and its significance will not be clear. It may be helpful, therefore, to take time this week to study the temple in the days of Jesus.

During Holy Week it is also important to see the cross from the perspective of the love that God has for us. Jesus' death on the cross shows us how much God loves us, for as St. Paul said, nothing can separate us from the love of God (Rom. 8:38-39). It is because we share Christ's victory over sin and death that we face the cross with feelings of sadness and remorse, but also with deep thankfulness for what we have been given. Good Friday is about triumph.

The tension between suffering and glorious triumph is set immediately before us on Palm Sunday, when joyful hosannas ring out even as the sense of foreboding grows. Jesus enters Jerusalem proclaimed as a king, riding toward a destiny of suffering and death amid the shouts of those who soon will turn against him.

Maundy Thursday recalls the Last Supper, when Jesus commanded his disciples and us to do two things—the two things he did in the Upper Room. He broke bread with them, saying, "Do this in remembrance of me" (Luke 22:19); in the eucharist we have the promise of his presence with us always. When he washed the disciples' feet, he commanded them to follow his example to love and humbly serve one another: "I give you a new commandment, that you love one another" (John 13:34).

Holy Saturday is a time for reflecting upon Jesus' death and burial and what it means for our lives. It is the calm after the storm as we await the sunrise.

## Great Words of Holy Week

| | |
|---|---|
| Atonement | Holy Mysteries |
| Broken bread | Humility |
| Calvary | Lash |
| Crown of thorns | Last Supper |
| Crucifix | Night watch |
| Crucifixion | Passion |
| Cup of wine | Redemption |
| Denial of Peter | Remembrance |
| Footwashing | Suffering |

Gethsemane              Tomb (sepulcher)
Golgotha                Trial before Pilate
Hosanna                 Way of the cross

## Holy Week Through the Eyes of a Child

- When Jesus rode into Jerusalem on the back of a donkey, the people who greeted him expected a powerful hero. They did not understand that Jesus' power was not physical strength, but the power of love.
- Jesus showed us that we are to remember him and follow his example of caring for and serving others. We remember him in the eucharist when we know he is present with us. We see his example of humbly serving others in love in his washing of the disciples' feet.
- Jesus proclaimed God's forgiveness from the cross as he was dying. He forgave Peter, who had denied him, and those who caused his death, and he will forgive us for all that we do that hurts others. That's why Good Friday is good.
- As God was with Jesus in his suffering, he is with us when we suffer.

## Symbols and Traditions of Holy Week

- Color—red (crimson); or purple as in Lent.
- Palms—fronds for the Procession on Palm Sunday. The people in Jerusalem waved them joyously as we might wave flags in a parade. As the rubric on page 270 of the Prayer Book points out, branches can be from local trees or shrubs.
- Donkey—the "colt of an ass" on which Jesus rode into Jerusalem; symbol of humility.
- Bowl and towel—reminders of Jesus' act of washing the disciples' feet; symbols of service and humility.
- Rooster—reminder of Peter's denial of Jesus before the cock crowed.
- Tenebrae—a monastic office of readings and music based on the Lamentations of Jeremiah, kept on Wednesday night of Holy Week in some parishes (see *The Book of Occasional Services*).
- Silencing of the organ—some parishes silence the organ from the Maundy Thursday liturgy until the *Gloria* at the Easter Vigil.

- Stripping of the altar—traditionally the altar is stripped and washed and the sanctuary is cleared after the eucharist on Maundy Thursday. No hangings remain until the Easter Vigil.
- Watch on Maundy Thursday—after the stripping of the altar an all-night watch is kept, usually with the reserved sacrament, just as Jesus prayed in the garden of Gethsemane.
- Crown of thorns—a Good Friday symbol (from Matthew 27:29 and John 19:2) because the soldiers mocked Jesus as a king, dressing him in a purple robe and placing a crown of thorns on his head.
- Crucifix cross—the image of the crucified Jesus upon the cross is a Good Friday symbol of suffering.
- Dogwood—according to legend, the dogwood, with its cross-shaped blossom marked as though with nail prints, may have been the tree used to build the cross.
- Lamb—Jesus, called the Lamb of God, was sacrificed like a Passover lamb: "Christ our Passover is sacrificed for us" (BCP 364).
- Sand dollar—a legendary symbol of Good Friday because of the five wounds of Jesus which appear to be depicted on it: four nail marks and the mark of the soldier's spear (John 19:34).
- Holy Saturday—as noted in the rubric for that day, this is the only day in the church year on which there is no communion, only a Liturgy of the Word (BCP 283) to ponder as we await the third day.

## Social Justice Themes for Holy Week

Two collects heard during Holy Week set the focus for social justice:
- Palm Sunday
  *Mercifully grant that we may walk in the way of his suffering.* (BCP 272)
- Monday in Holy Week
  *Almighty God, whose most dear Son went not up to joy but first he suffered pain, and entered not into glory before he was crucified: Mercifully grant that we, walking in the way of the cross, may find it none other than the way of life and peace.* (BCP 220)

These collects remind us that we are called:
- to identify with the suffering peoples of the nation and the world and not to remain aloof;
- to have compassion for "all sorts and conditions" of people (BCP 814).

| Story | Matthew | Mark | Luke | John |
|---|---|---|---|---|
| Triumphal entry into Jerusalem | 21:1-11 | 11:1-11 | 19:28-40 | 12:12-19 |
| Anointing at Bethany | 26:6-13 | 14:3-9 | | 12:1-8 |
| Cleansing of the temple | | 11:15-19 | 19:45-46 | |
| Conspiracy against Jesus | 26:1-5 | 14:1-2 | 19:47-48; 22:1-2 | 11:45-53 |
| Betrayal by Judas | 26:14-16, 20-25, 47-50 | 14:10-11, 17-22, 43-46 | 22:3-6, 21-23, 47-48 | 13:1-2, 18-30; 18:1-5 |
| Footwashing | | | | 13:3-17 |
| The Lord's Supper | 26:26-29 | 14:22-25 | 22:14-23 | |
| Peter's denial | 26:31-35, 69-75 | 14:26-31, 66-72 | 22:31-34, 54-62 | 13:36-38: 18:15-18, 25-27 |
| Jesus in Gethsemane | 26:36-46 | 14:32-42 | 22:39-46 | 18:1 |
| Jesus arrested | 26:47-56 | 14:43-52 | 22:47-53 | 18:2-12 |
| Jesus before Caiaphas | 26:57-68 | 14:53-65 | 22:54, 63-71 | 18:13-14, 19-24 |
| Jesus before Pilate | 27:1-2, 11-14 | 15:1-5 | 23:1-5 | 18:28-38a |
| Jesus before Herod | | | 23:6-12 | |
| Jesus sentenced to die | 27:15-26 | 15:6-15 | 23:13-25 | 18:38b– 19:16 |
| Jesus mocked | 27:27-31 | 15:16-20 | | 19:2-3 |
| The road to Golgotha | 27:32 | 15:21 | 23:26-32 | 19:17 |
| Jesus' crucifixion and death | 27:33-56 | 15:22-41 | 23:33-49 | 19:18-30 |
| Jesus' burial | 27:57-61 | 15:42-47 | 23:50-56 | 19:31-42 |
| The guard at the tomb | 27:62-66 | | | |

## Great Hymns of Holy Week

### Palm Sunday
- All glory, laud, and honor (Hymns 154, 155).

### Maundy Thursday
- Now my tongue, the mystery telling (Hymns 329, 330, 331).

### Good Friday
- Where charity and love prevail *(Ubi caritas)* (Hymn 581);
- Alone thou goest forth, O Lord (Hymn 164);
- Sing, my tongue, the glorious battle (Hymns 165, 166).


## Holy Week in *The Book of Common Prayer*

### Services with Holy Week Themes
- Proper Liturgies for Holy Week:
    - —Palm Sunday (BCP 270-273);
    - —Maundy Thursday (BCP 274-275);
    - —Good Friday (BCP 276-282);
    - —Holy Saturday (BCP 283);
- The Reconciliation of a Penitent (BCP 447-452);
- Ministration to the Sick (BCP 453-461);
- The Burial of the Dead (BCP 491-505).


## Living Holy Week at Home and in the Parish
- Making dioramas or arranging several rooms as scenes from the main events of Holy Week can clarify our understanding of the happenings they portray. A guided tour or narration can explain the scenes to visitors.
- A crown of thorns can be made by soaking stems of a plant with thorns until they are pliable enough to shape. Wire or tie the ends together to hold the shape as the stems dry out. Use the symbol in worship or in a place of meditation.
- Make a large wooden cross to be used as the rubric for the Good Friday liturgy indicates (BCP 281).

- A tape recording could give the details of Jesus' way to Calvary as a radio or television reporter might describe them.
- Make a list of every adjective you can think of that might describe the feelings of those who were witnesses to the Holy Week events. Share times when you have had similar feelings.
- Using gestures in silence, act out a Holy Week hymn, such as "Alone thou goest forth, O Lord" (Hymn 164).
- Bend large nails or palms to make small crosses for Holy Week devotions.
- Study the various kinds of crosses throughout Christian history to make examples for display.
- Encourage parents to participate in the services of the Triduum (Maundy Thursday through Easter Sunday) and the Easter Vigil. Children can be deeply touched by the music and rites of the services.
- Organize all-night prayer vigils with one-hour shifts, starting with the end of the Maundy Thursday service and ending with the Easter Vigil. Here again, children can be involved even if they simply sit with parents and read a book. They will remember the quiet and the commitment evidenced in such moments of devotion.

# The Days of Holy Week

## An Overview of Holy Week

Holy Week is an entering into Jesus' death through baptism so that "just as Christ was raised from the dead by the glory of the Father, so we too might walk in newness of life" (Rom. 6:4b).

The origins of Holy Week are found in the practices of Cyril, Bishop of Jerusalem, who died in 386; fortunately, these practices were witnessed and recorded by a pilgrim nun named Egeria.[1] As pilgrims poured into the holy city for their baptism on Easter Sunday morning, Cyril would lead them out to sites that were significant to the events leading up to Golgotha. With prayer, a dramatic reading of the story associated with the place, the

---

1   For excerpts from Egeria's writings, see *Readings for the Daily Office from the Early Church,* ed. J. Robert Wright (New York: Church Hymnal Corporation, 1991).

singing of hymns, and symbolic actions, these events were experienced again by the pilgrims. By the time of their baptism, Paul's powerful words of dying in order to have new life could be appreciated. They were truly raised with Christ, they felt, because they had walked through his death in their baptism.

Bishop Cyril should be honored as the patron saint of church educators! He knew the importance of the Christian story in forming a people, and he moved it right into their lives by involving them in experiences of drama, worship, and prayer during Holy Week. Later, during the Great Fifty Days of Easter, he helped the newly baptized reflect on the meaning of those stories for their new life in Jesus Christ.

Holy Week becomes an "in-house" retreat for candidates and their sponsors for baptism or the reaffirmation of their baptismal vows. They take part in prayer vigils, prepare the Maundy Thursday meal, participate in the footwashing, read the biblical texts at the Easter Vigil, and so forth.

## Palm Sunday, All Years

Lections: *At the Liturgy of the Palms:* Matthew 21:1-11 (Year A); Mark 11:1-11a (Year B); Luke 19:29-40 (Year C). *At the Liturgy of the Word:* Isaiah 45:21-25 or 52:13–53:12; Psalm 22:1-21; Philippians 2:5-11; The Passion from Matthew (Year A), Mark (Year B), or Luke (Year C)

**Event recalled in the lections**
*Liturgy of the Palms:* Jesus' entry into Jerusalem;
*Liturgy of the Word:* Jesus' passion and death on the cross.

## Monday in Holy Week

Lections: Isaiah 42:1-9; Psalm 36:5-10; Hebrews 11:39–12:3; John 12:1-11 or Mark 14:3-9

**Event recalled in the lections**
The anointing of Jesus. In John, Mary anoints Jesus "for his burial"; in Mark, the woman is unnamed. In both texts a woman anoints Jesus with

expensive perfume. Jesus understood this as symbolizing the anointing of his body for burial, which he knew would be soon.

## Tuesday in Holy Week

Lections: Isaiah 49:1-6; Psalm 71:1-12; 1 Corinthians 1:18-31; John 12:37-38, 42-50 or Mark 11:15-19

### Event recalled in the lections
*John:* a summary of Jesus' final teachings;
*Mark:* Jesus cleansing the temple.

## Wednesday in Holy Week

Lections: Isaiah 50:4-9a; Psalm 69:7-15, 22-23; Hebrews 9:11-15, 24-28; John 13:21-35 or Matthew 26:1-5, 14-25

### Event recalled in the lections
Judas' betrayal of Jesus: "And from that moment he began to look for an opportunity to betray him" (Matt. 26:16).

## Maundy Thursday

Lections: Exodus 12:1-14a; Psalm 78:14-20, 23-25; 1 Corinthians 11:23-26 (27-32); John 13:1-15 or Luke 22:14-30

### Event recalled in the lections
The Last Supper, including the footwashing in John.

## Good Friday

Lections: Isaiah 52:13–53:12 or Genesis 22:1-18 or Wisdom 2:1, 12-24; Psalm 22:1-21 or Psalm 22:1-11 or Psalm 40:1-14 or Psalm 69:1-23; Hebrews 10:1-25; John (18:1-40) 19:1-37

### Event recalled in the lections
Jesus' passion and death.

## Holy Saturday

Lections: Job 14:1-14; Psalm 130 or Psalm 31:1-5; 1 Peter 4:1-8; Matthew 27:57-66 or John 19:38-42

### Event recalled in the lections
The burial of Jesus.

# *Easter*

## Definition

Easter is a festival season of fifty days whose first day is Easter Day, the Sunday of the Resurrection, and whose last day is the Day of Pentecost. Easter begins after sundown on Holy Saturday. The celebration of Easter is initiated with the Easter Vigil, which can be observed after sundown but ideally is kept just before sunrise, so that the proclamation of Jesus' resurrection comes with the dawn of the new day. The Easter season includes the events of Christ's resurrection and ascension and the coming of the Holy Spirit on the Day of Pentecost.

- Easter Day is the principal feast of the church year.
- The word "Easter" comes from *Eostre,* a Teutonic goddess whose name is associated with springtime, growth, and fertility. In most languages the name of the day is *Pascha,* which means "Passover."
- Pentecost (from the Greek, meaning "fiftieth day") is the Christian feast that comes fifty days after Easter. The time between Easter and Pentecost is known as the Great Fifty Days.

## Holy Days in Easter

It is necessary to check the Calendar of the Church Year (BCP 15-33) for the holy days, lesser feasts, or other special observances that occur during the Easter season in a particular year.

## Easter Themes

The resurrection means that Christ has overcome death and in his victory has opened to us everlasting life. Nothing can separate us from the love of God (Rom. 8:38-39). New life—the Lord's new life in which we share—is the message of this season.

- As the sacrament of new life, baptism is an Easter theme; as baptized Christians we take time during Easter to ponder the meaning of membership in Christ's body, the church. We look at events in the church's life—the sacraments, the accounts of resurrection and the post-resurrection appearances of Jesus—to discover their meaning and what they tell us about how we as a community are to live the life of the Risen Lord.
- The word from the ancient tradition of the church to describe the Easter season is *Mystagogia*. This is the time when the "mysteries" of the sacraments, particularly baptism and eucharist, are revealed to the recently baptized.
- After the Lord is glorified in the ascension, he is present in a new way to the church in the gift of the Holy Spirit at Pentecost.
- Like the two who walked the Emmaus road with Jesus, we can know Christ in the sharing of the word and in the breaking of bread at the eucharist.

## Great Words of Easter

| | |
|---|---|
| Alleluia! | New life (renewal) |
| Christ is risen! | Newly baptized |
| Empty tomb | Paschal Mystery |
| Everlasting life | Promise |
| Hope | Reconciliation |
| Joy | Resurrection |
| Love | Victory |

## Easter Through the Eyes of a Child

- Jesus is risen from the dead! Easter has brought us everlasting life because of Jesus' resurrection.
- God's love is stronger than anything, even death. Because of God's love, we do not have to be afraid of death.
- Easter is about new life, coming from what we thought was death and bringing unexpected possibilities and surprises.
- We received new life at our baptism, and during Easter we think about what that baptism means in our lives.

- Color—white for festival and joy.
- The paschal candle—the darkness of death giving way to light and life, symbolizing Jesus' passing over from death into life. Also symbolizes the light of Creation, the pillar of fire that led the Israelites through the wilderness, the fire of Pentecost. *Pascha* is Greek for "Passover." The paschal candle is lit from Easter through the Day of Pentecost. The year's date is carved into the candle to show that the Good News of Easter is for every age, including us today.
- The Exsultet is a song of praise and joy sung at the lighting of the paschal candle at the beginning of the Easter Vigil (BCP 286).
- The Easter Vigil captures all of the powerful story imagery of Easter—which is why this service is so important in the life of the congregation. In planning the vigil, keep children as well as adults in mind. The readings (as few as two or as many as nine) can be offered by storytellers, as dramatic readings, or in dramatic presentations. Have the congregation move from a place of sharing the great stories of the faith to another place for baptism, and finally to the Holy Table for the proclamation of the resurrection and the celebration of the Holy Eucharist.
- A customary Easter greeting that Christians have used for centuries:
  *Leader:* "Alleluia! Christ is risen!"
  *Response:* "The Lord is risen indeed! Alleluia!"
- Baptisms and confirmations have traditionally occurred in this season of initiation. Ideally these sacraments take place at the Great Vigil of Easter.
- Feasting—breaking the fast of Lent with a feast is a sign of celebration and symbolizes the joy of the Christian community at Easter.
- The empty cross—a sign of the victory of Easter.
- Alleluias and the *Gloria*—joyful acclamations from the Easter community.
- Butterfly—symbolizes resurrection or new life from a cocoon.
- Egg—the Easter symbol from which new life emerges.
- Pomegranate—a regal symbol, filled with red seeds that further symbolize life and fertility and the open tomb.
- Ear of corn—as it bursts open we see the fertile new life within.
- Easter lily—symbol of purity and of beautiful new life.
- Each Sunday is a "little Easter," reminding us as Christians of the resurrection, since it was on the first day of the week that Jesus rose

from the dead. The joy of each weekly remembrance of the resurrection is always maintained, even during penitential seasons.

## Social Justice Themes for Easter

The collect for the Third Sunday of Easter asks God to "open the eyes of our faith, that we may behold him in all his redeeming work" (BCP 224). It reminds us that:

- the actions of the church and of individual Christians must be judged as to whether they are redeeming or demeaning works;
- the healing ministry of the church involves the healing of society as well as individuals.

The lections for the Fifth Sunday of Easter, Year B tell the story of Philip baptizing an Ethiopian eunuch, which is a reminder that no one is excluded in the church. A eunuch was considered unclean, but Philip did not hesitate to baptize him (Acts 8:26-40).

## Great Bible Stories for Easter

See individual Bible readings listed in connection with each Sunday in the Easter season.

## Great Hymns of Easter

Easter hymns 174-213, including:

- Hail, thee, festival day! (Hymn 175, Easter version);
- The strife is o'er, the battle done (Hymn 208);
- He is risen, he is risen! (Hymn 180).

## Easter in *The Book of Common Prayer*

### *Services with Easter Themes*

- The Great Vigil of Easter (BCP 285-295);
- The Burial of the Dead (BCP 491-505; note especially the rubric on BCP 507).

- Banners with the many symbols of Easter add to our mood of celebration and joy.
- Remembering the "gardener" who met Mary on that morning of the third day (John 20:15), make a garden by the church or tend the church yard. Planting seeds or bulbs or trees reminds us of Easter's new life. Think about window boxes or perhaps "dish gardens" to be given to those who are homebound.
- Make a simple sculpture with wire and pliers to depict the joy of Easter, resurrection, and new life.
- An egg tree (decorated Easter eggs that have been "blown" and tied to a tree branch) can be used for a table centerpiece or classroom or home decoration.
- Eggshell mosaics can illustrate an Easter story or symbols. Wash eggshells and arrange eggshell pieces on poster paper with white glue to make a design or picture. Use plain or colored shells, adding color if desired, either before or after gluing. Mosaics could also be used to make Easter cards or boxes for decorative gift containers.
- Slides, photographs, or pictures cut from magazines can be made into collages, posters, or booklets to illustrate experiences of death and resurrection in our lives. An assignment to capture such Easter experiences could make photographers of any age alert to everyday events that express this season. A "live" or taped narration or musical background could accompany the presentation.
- Easter cards can be made by hand or with computers, using any sort of lettering or drawings. Make potato-print stamps with Easter symbols on them by marking the design on the cut end of half a potato and scraping the background away, then placing the "stamp" on a sponge pad of poster paint or food coloring. Yarn, ribbon, string, leaves, or small flowers glued onto construction paper can also convey an Easter message.
- A triptych (made like a three-sided stained glass window) illustrating Palm Sunday, Good Friday, and Easter could be used in worship.
- Symbols of new life—eggs, butterflies, ears of corn, lilies, empty crosses—can be created in a great variety of sizes from all sorts of materials and recycled scraps. Hang them in spots all over church or home for an Easter celebration.
- Make kites with Easter symbols on them and enjoy flying them, remembering their symbolism of freedom and release.

# The Easter Vigil

## An Overview of the Easter Vigil

The Easter Vigil is the most important service of the Christian year. In the early church the catechumens, their sponsors, and catechists gathered for an all-night storytelling session that culminated in baptism, the proclamation of the resurrection, and the eucharist. The baptisms were by total immersion. As candidates were lowered into the water, they would remember the words about dying with Christ in baptism so that they could be raised with Christ in his resurrection. They were given white robes to wear after their immersion and anointing and then were led out to the congregation for the Holy Eucharist.

Such an event would have had a powerful effect. Today the drama and significance of baptism can be emphasized in a number of ways. Many congregations have all-night "lock-ins" with youth groups, and Easter sunrise services are already a standard practice in churches around the world. Consider holding an all-night storytelling time with candidates for baptism or reaffirmation. Gather the rest of the congregation together a half hour before sunrise for the full vigil service.

The Easter Vigil is an event in which the church tells the salvation story again with the candidates for baptism, summarizing the whole story as people prepare to turn their lives around. The message of the nine readings appointed from the Bible (though as few as two can be read) can be lost if they are read one after another interspersed only with psalms and prayers, but can be offered dramatically in a variety of ways to encourage the joyful participation and reflection of the people gathered.

The nine readings from the Vigil are outlined below, listed as "chapters" in salvation history. Along with the biblical citations are suggestions for sharing the texts at the vigil. These suggestions are offered only to stimulate your own imagination. Consider the gifts of your congregation; music, dance, dramatic reading, storytelling, visual arts, and poetry are but a few of the talents that can be exercised in the Great Vigil of Easter.

At the end of the fourth "chapter" in the salvation story, the texts move from remembering God's past deeds done on behalf of God's people and turn to the future promises of God. There is a dramatic shift here from "remember what God has done" to "hear what God is going to do." Without the memory, the future vision has no meaning. Only as the people of Israel recall the past actions of God can they have confidence in God's promises for the future.

A movement from one space to another might heighten the sense of this dramatic shift. Example: Offer the first four readings around the baptismal font to emphasize the memories associated with God's past actions. Three of the four memories include water imagery, making the font as a focal point particularly appropriate. Move to the altar for the five promises, since it represents the promise of the kingdom of God that is coming: "For I tell you that from now on I will not drink of the fruit of the vine until the kingdom of God comes" (Luke 22:18). The places where the vigil readings are offered do not have to be in the nave or sanctuary. Use the parish hall, an area out of doors, the columbarium, or other places that make sense in light of the texts.

## Chapters in the Salvation Story of the Easter Vigil

### Chapter 1: *Genesis 1:1–2:2 (The story of Creation)*
Read the text as a poem, with one person taking the part of the narrator and the other the part of God. At the end of each "day" in the text, invite the congregation to repeat the refrain, "Good. Good. Very, very good!"

### Chapter 2: *Genesis 7:1-5, 11-18, 8:6-18, 9:8-13 (The Flood)*
Read this text as a choral reading, assigning parts to two or more persons.

### Chapter 3: *Genesis 22:1-18 (Abraham's sacrifice of Isaac)*
Encourage an informal telling of the story rather than a reading from the Bible, thus capturing the way this text was shared in ancient times. A second alternative is to offer the story as a dramatic reading with persons taking the parts of the narrator, Abraham, and Isaac.

This is a reading that many of us would rather leave out of the Easter Vigil! How could the God we know in Jesus possibly have "tested" Abraham in such a way? Jews and Christians over many generations have been bothered by that very question, but they have also seen in this story the faith of the patriarch Abraham who trusted God to do what had to be done for the salvation of a people. Abraham's response is not unlike Mary's recorded in Luke: "Here am I, the servant of the Lord; let it be with me according to your word" (Luke 1:38a). Christians see in this story a direct connection to the death of God's beloved Son on the cross. The cross on Jesus' back was foreshadowed in the wood for the fire that Isaac carried up the hill.

### Chapter 4: *Exodus 14:10–15:1 (Israel's deliverance at the Red Sea)*

Here is a second opportunity for storytelling. Do not worry about including every word of the text in the telling of the story; shape the story in a way that makes it easier to tell. Again, a dramatic reading of the text is an excellent option. Movement as well as oral interpretation can be included: let Moses' arm be raised over the waters of the sea, and have several people move across the space with a sense of awe and wonder.

### Chapter 5: *Isaiah 4:2-6 (God's Presence in a renewed Israel)*

Offer as a choral reading, with two or more people reading in unison.

### Chapter 6: *Isaiah 55:1-11 (Salvation offered freely to all)*

If there are two readers, have the first reader offer Isaiah 55:1-5, with the second reader taking verses 6 through 11. (The second segment of this text is printed on page 86 of *The Book of Common Prayer* as Canticle 10, "The Second Song of Isaiah.")

### Chapter 7: *Ezekiel 36:24-28 (A new heart and a new spirit)*

The imagery of this prophetic promise invites dramatic movement. Consider asking someone who signs for those who are hearing impaired to express the text in sign language while someone else reads aloud.

### Chapter 8: *Ezekiel 37:1-14 (The valley of the dry bones)*

Here is a text that cries out for a dramatic rendering. The whole group could be drawn into the acting out of the reading. Have some participants lie on the floor as "dried bones." Put people in the four corners of the space to "breathe upon these slain, that they may live" (Ezek. 37:9b). They rise up as the breath of the Spirit is proclaimed from the four corners of the earth. If lying down on the floor is not practical, have people sit with eyes closed so that they hear the words of the spirit coming from all around them.

**Chapter 9: *Zephaniah 3:12-20 (The gathering of God's people)***
Have a single voice read the first two verses. Ask everyone to read the remainder of the text together in unison. If you have done the vigil readings outside the nave, the text is an invitation for the people to move in procession into the nave for baptism and the proclamation of the gospel: "At that time I will bring you home, at the time when I gather you" (Zeph. 3:20a).

# The Great Fifty Days of Easter

## An Overview of the Great Fifty Days

The Great Fifty Days of Easter, beginning with Easter Week, are the time when those who have reaffirmed their baptismal vows or have been baptized at the Easter Vigil reflect on the meaning of their baptism. Through the lectionary texts they explore the "mysteries" of their faith. The early church called this period of the process *mystagogia*. Today the whole church enters into this period of uncovering anew the mysteries of faith expressed in sacrament, word, and life lived for others. Each time we celebrate the Holy Eucharist using Eucharistic Prayer A, we say these words:

*We proclaim the mystery of faith:*

*Christ has died. Christ is risen. Christ will come again.* (BCP 363)

Some overall themes need to be kept in mind as the Great Fifty Days unfold.
- The role of the church is to continue the proclamation of the resurrection expressed with such joy at that first Easter. We hear the proclamation of the resurrection in order to pass on the good news.
- In a sense, Christ rose again *within* the church. Through the Holy Spirit, the risen Christ is revealed in every new generation. The apostles found themselves filled with the power to continue the acts of Jesus that revealed God's presence: Peter healed the man at the Beautiful Gate (Acts 3:1-10); "Many signs and wonders were done among the people through the apostles" (Acts 5:12a); Philip unfolded the meaning of God's word to the Ethiopian eunuch on the road to Gaza (Acts 8:26-39).
- The Great Fifty Days traditionally were a time when the mysteries of the faith were revealed to the recently baptized. The meaning of all

that the candidates experienced in Holy Week and the Easter Vigil unfolds in this time of intense theological reflection on just what it means to live as a covenant people.

- For congregations involved in the catechumenal process, the Great Fifty Days are a time of reflection on baptism. "What difference does my baptism make?" ask the recently baptized as they gather with priest, catechist, sponsor, and those who have reaffirmed their baptismal covenant.

- A question to ask each week: How will *we* know the risen Christ in our lives today?

## ◆ ◆ Year A ◆ ◆

### The Weeks of Easter, Year A

Sequential readings from the Acts of the Apostles are read during the Great Fifty Days because we need to hear the story of the first-century church in order to understand our mission in the church of today. In the Acts of the Apostles, the followers of Jesus suddenly realize that through the Holy Spirit they have the power to heal, to preach, to turn lives around, to witness to the presence of God and the coming reign of God in the world.

A course of readings from 1 Peter is heard each Sunday of the weeks of Easter in Year A. Some scholars believe that this letter is actually an early baptismal rite that included exhortations, sermons, and so forth. Thus we are formed during Easter with the same understanding of baptism that was given to the earliest converts.

Alternative selections from the Hebrew scriptures that are in thematic harmony with the gospel lections or with the Easter themes are provided in all three years. When the Hebrew scripture selection is used, it replaces either the reading from Acts or the reading from 1 Peter.

### Easter Sunday, Year A
The Resurrection of Jesus the Christ is proclaimed (John 20:1-10 [11-18] or Matthew 28:1-10).

## The Second Sunday of Easter, Year A

The story of Jesus appearing to Thomas (John 20:19-31).

*Theme of the lections*

Knowing the risen Christ through faith.

*How will the risen Christ be known in the generations to come?*

We may not *see* the risen Christ but we will *know* the risen Christ as we gather in faith-filled community on the "eighth day."

*Blessed are those who have not seen and yet have come to believe.* (John 20:29b)

## The Third Sunday of Easter, Year A

The disciples on the road to Emmaus (Luke 24:13-35).

*Theme of the lections*

Sacramental life.

*How will the risen Christ be known in the generations to come?*

The risen Christ is known in the sharing of the word and in the breaking of bread. This text reflects the form of the eucharist celebrated each week in the congregation: the Liturgy of the Word and the Liturgy at the Table.

*Lord Jesus, stay with us, for evening is at hand and the day is past; be our companion in the way, kindle our hearts, and awaken hope, that we may know you as you are revealed in Scripture and the breaking of bread. Grant this for the sake of your love.* (BCP 124)

## The Fourth Sunday of Easter, Year A

Jesus as the Good Shepherd (John 10:1-10).

*Theme of the lections*

Ministry as a way of revealing the risen Christ.

*How will the risen Christ be known in the generations to come?*

The risen Christ is known through the ministry of the church modeled by Jesus, the Good Shepherd.

## The Fifth Sunday of Easter, Year A

Jesus is the way to the Father (John 14:1-14).

*Theme of the lections*

One cannot be Christian alone; apart from the Body we can do nothing.

♦ To know the risen Christ is to be expectant: "I go to prepare a place for you" (John 14:2b) and "I am the way, and the truth, and the life" (John 14:6b).

- To know Jesus is to know the Father: "Whoever has seen me has seen the Father" (John 14:9b).
- The church and Christ are one: "Very truly, I tell you, the one who believes in me will also do the works that I do" (John 14:12a).

*How will the risen Christ be known in the generations to come?*

The church will reveal the risen Christ to the world and to each other through the community of faithful gathered and scattered as the Body of Christ. We are "made one body with him, that he may dwell in us, and we in him" (BCP 336).

### The Sixth Sunday of Easter, Year A

Jesus is the "true vine" (John 15:1-8).

*Theme of the lections*

Continued from Easter 5: One cannot be Christian alone; apart from the Body we can do nothing.

*How will the risen Christ be known in the generations to come?*

Continued from Easter 5: The church will reveal the risen Christ to the world and to each other through the community of faithful: "I am the vine, you are the branches. Those who abide in me and I in them bear much fruit, because apart from me you can do nothing" (John 15:5).

### The Seventh Sunday of Easter, Year A

Jesus prays for his disciples (John 17:1-11).

*Theme of the lections*

The church consecrated as the Body of Christ.

*How will the risen Christ be known in the generations to come?*

The Holy Spirit empowers the church. The text for this Sunday might be called a "Prayer of Consecration" for the church. The Body of Christ becomes a living sacrament to the world, an "outward and visible sign" of Christ's redeeming presence in history.

> *The words that you gave to me I have given to them, and they have received them and know in truth that I came from you; and they have believed that you sent me....And now I am no longer in the world, but they are in the world, and I am coming to you. Holy Father, protect them in your name that you have given me, so that they may be one, as we are one. (John 17:8, 11)*

# ♦ ♦ Year B ♦ ♦

## The Weeks of Easter, Year B

As in Year A, in Year B we read selections from the Acts of the Apostles for the six weeks of Easter following Easter Sunday because we need to hear the story of the first-century church in order to understand our mission in the world today.

For the epistle lections in Year B we read selections from 1 John. This writing seems to have come out of the community that was influenced by the gospel of John. The concern of 1 John is to clarify the testimony given about Jesus in the gospel of John. Heresies were beginning to influence the church, and 1 John was written partly as a corrective to false teachings. In the Easter season, this sequential reading of 1 John provides us with reflections about our faith in Christ that guide us through this period of *mystagogia*.

Selections from the Hebrew scriptures are provided as alternatives in all three years. When the Hebrew scriptures are used, they replace either the selection from Acts or the selection from 1 John.

### Easter Sunday, Year B
The Resurrection of Jesus the Christ is proclaimed (Mark 16:1-8).

### The Second Sunday of Easter, Year B
The story of Jesus appearing to Thomas (John 20:19-31).
*Theme of the lections*
> We know the risen Christ through faith. "Blessed are those who have not seen and yet have come to believe" (John 20:29b). We may not *see* the risen Christ but we will *know* the risen Christ as we gather in faith-filled community on the "eighth day."

### The Third Sunday of Easter, Year B
The road to Emmaus (Luke 24:36b-48).
*Theme of the lections*
> We know Christ in sacramental life. Jesus appears to the disciples and in eating with them he is able to show that he appears not as a ghost but as the risen Christ. Then he opens "their minds to understand the

scriptures," relating what they have experienced with him to what they know of the Hebrew scriptures. This lection has a focus similar to the Emmaus story in Year A (see Easter 3, Year A).

### The Fourth Sunday of Easter, Year B

Jesus as the Good Shepherd (John 10:11-16).

*Theme of the lections*

The risen Christ is known through the ministry of the church modeled by Jesus, the Good Shepherd.

### The Fifth Sunday of Easter, Year B

The promise of the Holy Spirit (John 14:15-21).

*Theme of the lections*

A new community is formed out of the resurrection; the indwelling of the Holy Spirit is the life of that community. Jesus promises his followers that those who love him will be guided by the Holy Spirit and will also see him. Jesus reminds his followers that though he will soon leave them in death, he will send them the Holy Spirit. Those who follow the commandments of love will find new life in intimate association with Jesus and the Father.

### The Sixth Sunday of Easter, Year B

Jesus tells his disciples to love one another (John 15:9-17).

*Theme of the lections*

The theme of the new community formed out of the resurrection and the indwelling of the Holy Spirit in the life of that community continues from Easter 5. Jesus speaks of his great love for his disciples, which has come to him from the Father, and calls upon them to show the same love toward each other. This love has formed his followers into a new community in relationship with Jesus and the Father, no longer servants but friends.

### The Seventh Sunday of Easter, Year B

Jesus prays for his disciples (John 17:11b-19).

*Theme of the lections*

The church is consecrated as the Body of Christ. The Holy Spirit empowers and sanctifies the church. The Body of Christ becomes a living sacrament to the world, an "outward and visible sign" of Christ's redeeming presence in history.

*Sanctify them in the truth; your word is truth. As you have sent me*
*into the world, so I have sent them into the world. And for their sakes*
*I sanctify myself, so that they also may be sanctified in truth.* (John
17:17-19)

❖ ❖ Year C ❖ ❖

## The Weeks of Easter, Year C

As in Year A and Year B, we read selections from the Acts of the Apostles
for the six weeks of Easter following Easter Sunday because we need to hear
the story of the first-century church in order to understand our mission in
the world today.

The second readings during the Great Fifty Days of Easter in Year C come
from the Revelation to John, providing glimpses of God's coming reign,
when Christ's work of reconciliation is fully realized. The readings from the
Hebrew scriptures can be substituted for the first or second reading during
Easter, though the tradition is to read only from the Christian scriptures
during this season.

### Easter Sunday, Year C
The Resurrection of Jesus the Christ is proclaimed (Luke 24:1-10).

### The Second Sunday of Easter, Year C
The story of Jesus appearing to Thomas (John 20:19-31).
#### Theme of the lections
Knowing the risen Christ through faith. "Blessed are those who have
not seen and yet have come to believe" (John 20:29b). We may not
see the risen Christ but we will *know* the risen Christ as we gather in
faith-filled community on the "eighth day."

### The Third Sunday of Easter, Year C
Jesus appears to the seven disciples by the Sea of Tiberias (John 21:1-14).
#### Theme of the lections
Knowing Christ in sacramental life. Jesus appears to the disciples and
in eating with them he is able to show that he appears not as a ghost

but as the risen Christ. This lection has a focus similar to the Emmaus story (see Easter 3, Year A).

### The Fourth Sunday of Easter, Year C
Jesus as the Good Shepherd (John 10:22-30).
> #### Theme of the lections
> Ministry as a way of revealing the risen Christ. The risen Christ is known through the ministry of the church modeled by Jesus, the Good Shepherd, who gives eternal life.

### The Fifth Sunday of Easter, Year C
The new commandment to love one another (John 13:31-35).
> #### Theme of the lections
> The new community formed out of the resurrection will be known by the love its members have for one another.

### The Sixth Sunday of Easter, Year C
Jesus promises the coming of the Holy Spirit (John 14:23-29).
> #### Theme of the lections
> The theme of the new community formed out of the resurrection continues from Easter 5. Jesus promises the Holy Spirit, who will come to be their counselor and dwell with them in their life together.

### The Seventh Sunday of Easter, Year C
Jesus prays for his disciples (John 17:20-26).
> #### Theme of the lections
> The unity of the church. We hear the conclusion of Jesus' great "priestly prayer," in which he calls for unity within the church so that Christians can witness to the presence of God in their lives.

# Ascension Day

## Definition

The Feast of the Ascension is celebrated forty days after Easter Sunday (therefore always on a Thursday) and recalls our Lord's exaltation by being taken gloriously up into heaven. After Jesus' crucifixion and resurrection, scripture tells us, he was seen for forty days before he ascended into heaven to be "seated at the right hand of God the Father." After Jesus' ascension, the disciples awaited the promised Spirit in Jerusalem.

## Ascension Themes

- The ascension is the third event in the cycle of crucifixion-resurrection-ascension in which our Lord's life on earth culminates with his being raised to live and reign gloriously with God forever.
- The ascended Christ is Lord of all, and we are charged by Christ to be witnesses, evangelizing the world in his name: individuals, institutions, communities, and nations.
- In the ascension Christ has taken our human nature into heaven where, as our advocate, he intercedes for us continually.

## Great Words of the Ascension

| | |
|---|---|
| Christ is Lord | Fulfillment |
| Crown of Life | Intercessor |
| Evangelize | King of Glory |
| Exaltation of human nature | Witness |

## The Ascension Through the Eyes of a Child

- We do not have to be afraid of dying because Jesus has gone ahead to prepare a place for us in heaven with those who love God.
- We know and feel real things we cannot see, like our parents' and friends' love.

## Symbols of Ascension Day

- Color—white, for festival and joy.
- Crown—symbol of the reign of our Lord Jesus Christ.

## Great Bible Stories for the Ascension

- The accounts of the ascension of Jesus: Mark 16:19; Luke 24:50-53; Acts 1:9-11.

## Great Hymns of the Ascension

Ascension hymns 214-222, including:
- Hail thee, festival day! (Hymn 216, Ascension version);
- The head that once was crowned with thorns (Hymn 483).

## Ascension Day, All Years

Lections: Acts 1:1-11; Psalm 47; Ephesians 1:15-23; Luke 24:49-53 or Mark 16:9-15, 19-20 (see BCP for alternative lessons)

### Theme of the lections

The risen Jesus is lifted up into heaven and no longer seen by the disciples.
- *Epistle:* Christ is the head of the church.

### Phrases for highlighting and memorization

- "Men of Galilee, why do you stand looking up toward heaven? This Jesus, who as been taken up from you into heaven, will come in the same way as you saw him go into heaven." (Acts 1:11)
- "God has gone up with a shout, the LORD with the sound of the ram's-horn." (Psalm 47:5)

- "[God] has put all things under [Christ's] feet and made him the head over all things for the church, which is his body, the fullness of him who fills all in all." (Eph. 1:22-23)
- "While he was blessing them, he withdrew from them and was carried up into heaven." (Luke 24:51)

### Key words, ideas, and concepts to explore

- authority;
- Christ as high priest;
- "seated at God's right hand";
- head of the church;
- kingdom or reign of God.

### Stories to tell

- The story of Christ's ascension from Luke and Acts.

### Christian practice and liturgical tradition

- Belief in Christ's ascension is an important element in the major creeds of the church.
- We pray to God "through Christ" as a recognition that Christ intercedes for us "at the right hand of the Father." The familiar refrain that closes many of our prayers and collects captures this image:

  *...through Jesus Christ our Lord, who lives and reigns with you and the Holy Spirit, one God, for ever and ever.*

### Formation in baptismal discipleship

The Baptismal Covenant affirms our belief that after his death and resurrection Jesus Christ "ascended into heaven, and is seated at the right hand of the Father" (BCP 304).

# The Day of Pentecost

## Definition

The Feast of Pentecost celebrates the day that the Holy Spirit came to the disciples as they were gathered together in Jerusalem. The Book of Acts tells us that the Holy Spirit was like the rush of a mighty wind, with tongues of flame like fire that rested on each person. After Easter, Pentecost is the second most important feast of the church.

"Pentecost" is from the Greek, meaning "fiftieth day." It was the Greek name for the Hebrew Feast of Weeks, which fell on the fiftieth day after Passover. Christians took this name because this was the same day that the Spirit descended upon the apostles. The Feast of Weeks celebrated the calling of the Hebrews into a covenant relationship with God at Mt. Sinai. With the coming of the Holy Spirit, the church realized a new covenant proclaimed by the prophet Jeremiah years before: "I will put my law within them, and I will write it on their hearts" (Jer. 31:33).

Another traditional name for the Feast of Pentecost is Whitsunday. This name probably comes from the white robes worn on the day of baptism (White-Sunday).

## Pentecost Themes

+ Christ the Lord, crucified, risen, and ascended, is present to the church through his Holy Spirit.

- Pentecost is the great and glorious climax of the Easter season, when the Holy Spirit gives power to the church through the apostles to spread the gospel to the ends of the earth.
- Pentecost is the fulfillment of Christ's promise that God would send the Spirit to be with us always and to give power to God's people (John 14:16).
- Pentecost is the birthday of the church, of the new covenant with God given to all believers.
- The author of Luke and Acts saw history as divided into three periods: the time of Israel and the prophets (with John the Baptist as the last prophet); the time of Jesus' earthly ministry; and the time of the church, which began at Pentecost and in which we are living now. Pentecost is the first event of the church's history.

## Great Words of Pentecost

| | |
|---|---|
| Apostles | Indwelling |
| Breath (sign of life) | Inspiration |
| Dove | Mighty wind |
| Empowered by the Spirit | New Covenant |
| Enthusiasm (Greek: filled with the Spirit) | Proclaiming |
| | Renewal |
| Evangelism | Tongues of fire |
| Gift of speech | Witnesses |

## Pentecost Through the Eyes of a Child

- God promises to be with us always.
- We are strengthened from within by the Holy Spirit, whose power, like a strong wind, we can feel even though we cannot see it.

## Symbols and Traditions of Pentecost

- Red—for the tongues of flame that signify the Holy Spirit.
- Descending dove—indicates the presence of divinity and the power of God working in people (see Matt. 3:16).
- Tongues of fire—an ancient symbol for divine presence.

- Lessons read in other languages at the eucharist—remind us of the variety of languages spoken on Pentecost.
- Mighty wind—felt and heard by the apostles; a symbol of the spirit (in Hebrew, Greek, and Latin, the words for "wind" and "spirit" are the same).
- Pentecost vigil—held at night or early in the morning using the Order of Worship for the Evening (BCP 109-114; see BCP 227, 896). The readings are the same for all three years of the lectionary.
- Baptisms and confirmations—traditionally part of both the Pentecost vigil and principal services, since Pentecost is one of the five "especially appropriate" days for baptism (BCP 312).
- The Easter Alleluias—used at worship on this final day of the Easter season.
- Wearing red clothing at worship services—to signify the tongues of fire of the Holy Spirit.

## Social Justice Themes for Pentecost

The Day of Pentecost opened the way of eternal life to every race and nation. On this day it is appropriate to study racism, sexism, and all other attitudes and actions that deny God's love for *all* people.

## Great Bible Stories for Pentecost

- Tower of Babel—confusion of languages (Genesis 11:1-9);
- Mount Sinai (Exodus 19, 20);
- The Spirit resting on the seventy elders of Israel in the wilderness with Moses (Numbers 11:24-30);
- Elijah and Elisha (2 Kings 2:1-15);
- Nicodemus (John 3:1-21);
- The Pentecost experience (Acts 2).

## Great Hymns of Pentecost

Pentecost hymns 223-230, including:
- Hail thee, festival day (Hymn 225, Pentecost version);
- Come thou Holy Spirit bright (Hymns 226, 227).

### Prayers and Thanksgivings for Pentecost

- Eucharistic Prayer D (BCP 372-376, from the Liturgy of St. Basil);
- Collect "For the Unity of the Church" (BCP 255);
- Collects II (BCP 256) and III (BCP 256-257) pray for the Spirit's help in choosing suitable persons for ordained ministry and for the vocation of all Christians.

### Services with Pentecost Themes

- Vigil of Pentecost (see BCP 227). The vigil begins with the Order of Worship for the Evening (BCP 109-114). Instead of the *Phos hilaron* we may substitute the *Gloria in excelsis* and a series of readings listed on pages 896, 906-907, or 917 of *The Book of Common Prayer*. The service concludes with the Holy Eucharist.
- Ordination rites (BCP 512-555).
- The Dedication and Consecration of a Church (BCP 567-574).

## Living Pentecost at Home and in the Parish

- Have a birthday party for the church with balloons and banners and a birthday cake, perhaps with doves or flames of fire on it. Think of red food—strawberries, punch.
- Make a gift for everyone attending the Pentecost service. Cut tongues of fire from red, orange, and yellow felt to pin on the shoulder.
- Have a celebration involving wind: make and use kites and pinwheels, fans, wind chimes, mobiles that move in the breeze, toy sailboats for races, parachutes, scarves that trail in the wind, a model windmill.

## The Day of Pentecost, All Years

Lections: Acts 2:1-11; Psalm 104:25-37; 1 Corinthians 12:4-13; John 20:19-23 or John 14:8-17 (See BCP for alternative lessons.)

### Theme of the lections

The gift of the Holy Spirit empowers Christians for ministry in the world.

*Phrases for highlighting and memorization*

- "All of them were filled with the Holy Spirit and began to speak in other languages, as the Spirit gave them ability." (Acts 2:4)
- "You send forth your Spirit, and they are created; and so you renew the face of the earth." (Psalm 104:31)
- "To each is given the manifestation of the Spirit for the common good." (1 Cor. 12:7)
- "When he had said this, he breathed on them and said to them, 'Receive the Holy Spirit.'" (John 20:22)
- "If you love me, you will keep my commandments. And I will ask the Father, and he will give you another Advocate, to be with you forever. This is the Spirit of truth, whom the world cannot receive, because it neither sees him nor knows him. You know him, because he abides with you, and he will be in you." (John 14:15-17)

*Key words, ideas, and concepts to explore*

- Holy Spirit;
- breath of God;
- empowered for ministry;
- varieties of gifts;
- speaking in other tongues.

*Stories to tell*

- Jesus' followers receiving the Holy Spirit in Acts and in John 20.

*Christian practice and liturgical tradition*

- The anointing with the Holy Spirit is a key point in the baptismal rite.
  *"N., you are sealed by the Holy Spirit in Baptism and marked as Christ's own for ever."* (BCP 308)
- At the ordination of a deacon, priest, or bishop, the ordaining bishop prays that the candidate will receive the Holy Spirit. The ancient hymn "Come, Holy Ghost, our souls inspire" is often sung at this point in the rite.
- The *Epiclesis,* or Invocation of the Holy Spirit, is an important part of every eucharistic prayer. Bread, wine, and the people of God are sanctified by the Holy Spirit. The sanctification of the faithful at the eucharist expresses the gift of the Holy Spirit received at baptism.
  *Sanctify them by your Holy Spirit to be for your people the Body and Blood of your Son, the holy food and drink of new and unending life*

*in him. Sanctify us also that we may faithfully receive this holy Sacrament, and serve you in unity, constancy, and peace.* (BCP 363)

### Formation in baptismal discipleship

The empowerment of the Holy Spirit must be a constant emphasis in the congregation. At baptism the Holy Spirit becomes a gift of ministry to each person, and the congregation must ensure that these gifts of the Spirit are raised up and nurtured.

# Trinity Sunday

## Definition

Trinity Sunday is the first Sunday after Pentecost. It celebrates the doctrine of the Trinity, the belief that God is revealed to us in three persons existing in a mutual relationship of love. Our understanding of the Trinity arises from the biblical, creedal, and doctrinal statements that emerged from the creative struggles of theologians in the church to understand and talk about the nature of God.

## Trinity Themes

- The Nicene and Apostles' creeds express our faith in God revealed to us as a Trinity of persons: God the Father, God the Son, and God the Holy Spirit.
- After the crucifixion-resurrection-ascension cycle of our Lord's life and the descent of the Holy Spirit on the apostles at Pentecost, the church celebrates the full revelation of God in the three persons of the Trinity.

## Great Words of Trinity Sunday

| | |
|---|---|
| Community | One-in-three |
| Creator | Persons |
| God the Father | Redeemer |
| God the Son | Sanctifier |
| God the Holy Spirit | Three-in-one |
| Mutual indwelling | Unity |

## Trinity Through the Eyes of a Child

We know God when:

- we see God's creation all around us;
- we learn of God's love for everyone from Jesus' life and teaching;
- we feel the power and strength of God's Spirit within us;
- we know God's love in the community of the church.

## Symbols and Traditions of Trinity Sunday

- Color—white, the color of joy.
- Equilateral triangle—three in one.
- Three interlocking circles—inseparability and unity.
- Blessing—the cross is signed in the name of the Father, Son, and Holy Spirit.
- We celebrate the Trinity in the *Gloria in excelsis.*
- All collects and many prayers end with ascription to the Holy Trinity.

## Great Hymns of Trinity Sunday

Trinity hymns 362-371, including:

- I bind unto myself today (Hymn 370);
- Come, thou almighty King (Hymn 365);
- Holy God we praise thy Name (Hymn 366);
- Thou, whose almighty word (Hymn 371).

## Trinity Sunday in *The Book of Common Prayer*

### Prayers and Thanksgivings

- The three prefaces of the Lord's Day (BCP 377-378) summarize our understanding of the three persons of the Trinity.
- The collect for Trinity Sunday (BCP 228).
- An additional collect concerning the Holy Trinity (BCP 251).

### Services with Trinity Themes

- Holy Baptism has a trinitarian emphasis throughout. Notice especially the Baptismal Covenant (BCP 304-305), the Thanksgiving over the Water (BCP 306-307), and the baptism itself (BCP 307-308).

- The prayer for renewal of the Baptismal Covenant said by the bishop before confirmation (BCP 309) refers to each of the persons of the Trinity in their relationship to the life of a committed Christian.
- The historic creeds that appear in the Prayer Book are sources of our understanding of the Trinity: the Apostles' Creed (BCP 96); the Nicene Creed (BCP 326-327); the Creed of St. Athanasius (BCP 864-865).

## Living Trinity Sunday at Home and in the Parish

- A banner or altar cloth can be made to express the theme of praise to the Trinity. A line from prayers or even an entire canticle could serve as the basis for these illustrations.
- "The Grace" from 2 Corinthians 13:13 is a text that lends itself to illustration in a number of ways, including poetry, sentence completion (such as "The fellowship of the Holy Spirit makes me think of ..."), hangings, sculptures, murals, and mobiles.
- Ask questions that will encourage people to talk about their experiences of God in different "persons," such as God as a loving parent, a forgiving savior, a strengthening companion.

## Trinity Sunday, Year A

Lections: Genesis 1:1–2:3; Psalm 150 or Canticle 2 or 13; 2 Corinthians 13:(5-10) 11-14; Matthew 28:16-20

### Theme of the lections
The God who creates, redeems, and sanctifies is revealed to us in three persons.

### Phrases for highlighting and memorization
- "In the beginning when God created the heavens and the earth, the earth was a formless void and darkness covered the face of the deep, while a wind from God swept over the face of the waters." (Gen. 1:1-2)
- "Let everything that has breath praise the LORD." (Psalm 150:6)
- "Glory to you, beholding the depths; in the high vault of heaven, glory to you." (Canticle 13)
- "The grace of the Lord Jesus Christ, the love of God, and the communion of the Holy Spirit be with all of you." (2 Cor. 13:13)

* "Go therefore and make disciples of all nations, baptizing them in the name of the Father and of the Son and of the Holy Spirit, and teaching them to obey everything that I have commanded you." (Matt. 28:19-20)

### Key words, ideas, and concepts to explore
* Trinity;
* names of God;
* God's power revealed in creation and history;
* creeds of the church.

### Christian practice and liturgical tradition
* "The Grace" from 2 Corinthians appears at the conclusion of both versions of Morning Prayer and Evening Prayer.
* Following Jesus' directive to his disciples in Matthew 28, Christians are baptized in the name of the Trinity.
    *N., I baptize you in the Name of the Father, and of the Son, and of the Holy Spirit.* (BCP 307)

### Formation in baptismal discipleship
The relationship of love among the three persons of the Trinity serves as a model for communities of baptized Christians living together in unity.

## Trinity Sunday, Year B
Lections: Exodus 3:1-6; Psalm 93 or Canticle 2 or 13; Romans 8:12-17; John 3:1-16

### Theme of the lections
The God of history is revealed in three persons: Father, Son, and Spirit.

### Phrases for highlighting and memorization
* "He said further, 'I am the God of your father, the God of Abraham, the God of Isaac, and the God of Jacob.' And Moses hid his face, for he was afraid to look at God." (Exod. 3:6)
* "Mightier than the sound of many waters, mightier than the breakers of the sea, mightier is the LORD who dwells on high." (Psalm 93:5)
* "Glory to you, beholding the depths; in the high vault of heaven, glory to you." (Canticle 13)

- "When we cry, 'Abba! Father!' it is that very Spirit bearing witness with our spirit that we are children of God, and if children, then heirs, heirs of God and joint heirs with Christ—if, in fact, we suffer with him so that we may also be glorified with him." (Rom. 8:15-17)
- "For God so loved the world that he gave his only Son, so that everyone who believes in him may not perish but may have eternal life." (John 3:16)

### Key words, ideas, and concepts to explore
- Trinity;
- names of God;
- Abba;
- burning bush;
- heirs with Christ.

### Stories to tell
- The story of God revealed to Moses in the burning bush.

### Formation in baptismal discipleship
The mutual and equal relationships among the three persons of the Trinity provide the basic model for understanding the church as community. As God is known in a communion of three persons, so the church is to be known as the community of God's people.

## Trinity Sunday, Year C
Lections: Isaiah 6:1-8; Psalm 29 or Canticle 2 or 13; Revelation 4:1-11; John 16:(5-11) 12-15

### Theme of the lections
The glory of the Lord is revealed in three persons through the Spirit of truth.

### Phrases for highlighting and memorization
- "Holy, holy, holy is the LORD of hosts; the whole earth is full of his glory." (Isaiah 6:3b)
- "The LORD shall give strength to his people; the LORD shall give his people the blessing of peace." (Psalm 29:11)

- "Glory to you, seated between the Cherubim; on the throne of your majesty, glory to you." (Canticle 13)
- "You are worthy, our Lord and God, to receive glory and honor and power, for you created all things, and by your will they existed and were created." (Rev. 4:11)
- "I still have many things to say to you, but you cannot bear them now. When the Spirit of truth comes, he will guide you into all the truth; for he will not speak on his own, but will speak whatever he hears, and he will declare to you the things that are to come." (John 16:12-13)

### Key words, ideas, and concepts to explore
- Trinity;
- names of God;
- glory;
- holy;
- Spirit of truth;
- seraphim and cherubim.

### Christian practice and liturgical tradition
- Part of the text of the *Sanctus,* which is sung or said at every eucharist, is taken from Isaiah 6.

### Formation in baptismal discipleship
Christians are called to be holy, as God is holy.

# The Season After Pentecost

## Definition

The numbered weeks after Pentecost are sometimes referred to as "Ordinary Time" because these weeks of the year are not associated with specific seasons, such as Lent and Easter, with their overriding themes. The Season after Pentecost begins with Trinity Sunday (the first Sunday after Pentecost) and ends on the last Sunday after Pentecost, just before Advent begins. The numbered proper to be used on each of the Sundays after Pentecost is determined by the calendar date of that Sunday (see BCP 158). The liturgical color for the Season after Pentecost is green, and these weeks during the summer and fall months in the Northern Hemisphere have often been connected with growth and fruitfulness in the Christian life.

## Holy Days in the Season after Pentecost

A number of saints' and holy days fall within this season, including:

- The Transfiguration of Our Lord Jesus Christ (August 6);
- Saint Mary the Virgin (August 15);
- Holy Cross Day (September 14);
- Saint Matthew, Apostle and Evangelist (September 21);
- Saint Luke the Evangelist (October 18);
- All Saints' Day (November 1).

## Themes in the Season after Pentecost

The Season after Pentecost does not have a single theme; rather, each week bears its own theme, usually based on the collect, first reading, and the reading from the gospel, since the epistle readings are sequential. In addition to focusing on the themes of each Sunday, it may be helpful to organize educational offerings during these months under four broad categories of the Christian life:

- Our relationship with God;
- Our relationship with Jesus Christ and with one another through our prayers, the sacraments, and life in the body of Christ;
- The presence of the Holy Spirit in our lives;
- The church and its mission.

## Education in the Summer Season

The summer Sundays after Pentecost bring a great gift: TIME.

- *Time* to do the important things that were put off because other seasons were too full to include them.
- *Time* to plan ahead and to meet with leaders and teachers for the coming year.
- *Time* to involve other leadership, giving church school teachers who have worked through the past year more opportunity for reading, leisure, rest, and prayer.
- *Time* for introducing special emphases.
- *Time* for fun together as a whole parish or as smaller groups: picnics, cookouts, overnight camping trips, swimming parties, outdoor suppers.

### Ideas for summer educational programs

Because summer is the time for family vacations, summer camp, and visits to friends and relatives who live in distant places, attendance is less regular and the patterns of parish Christian education usually change in summer. This should not be used as a rationale to shut down the educational program of the congregation, however. Most people do stay home for the bulk of the summer, but when programs are cut off for the season it becomes an invitation for people to drop out. Instead, change the pace of congregational life. Offer a variety of activities that say summer is different, but still a time for learning and discovery. Some ideas include:

- *Intergenerational activities and study* around a common theme. People of every age can be teachers and learners.
- *Interest Centers* designed around a central theme in one large room or separated in smaller rooms. The centers could be planned for adults and children of all ages or in specific groupings. Interest Centers might include:
    —Arts activities, such as painting, lettering, clay modeling, stitching, mobiles, photography, film making;
    —Creative writing, interviews, or news stories;
    —Simple creative drama, puppets, shadow plays or pantomime, choral readings, taping of sound effects;
    —Projects that will take several weeks, such as making banners, shields, research on a subject, displays, models or dioramas, field trips, outreach projects, nature or ecology activities;
    —Learning hymns or folk songs, exploring Christianity in the arts;
    —Take families and individuals to a local camp or conference site and spend the weekend together. Offer intergenerational and/or age grouped opportunities for worship, art and a variety of other activities.
- *A Vacation Church School* for a specified period, perhaps one or two weeks.
- *Meet in different locations and at different times* (such as outdoors, in each others' homes, at some place of recreation) for meals, overnight camping, or retreats.

### Ideas for summer projects
- Reenact the life of the early Christians. Build a house, make costumes, write scrolls, and have some of the saints of that time "visit."
- Build a house or town of the Holy Land.
- Build a puppet stage for use all year.
- Cook and enjoy some foods mentioned in the Bible.
- Plant an herb garden using the herbs mentioned in the Bible. Dry the herbs in the fall and use them for cooking or decorations.
- Relive the entire church year, Advent to Pentecost, devoting one or two days to each season, depending on the time available. A good idea for a summer camp program.
- Identify social justice issues in your community, the nation, or the world. Gather the information you need and invite local resource

people. Develop sessions for research, field trips, films, keeping in mind the question: How can we as Christians respond to the situation?

- ◆ Learn about how to participate in the mission activities of the larger church. Information about the Presiding Bishop's Fund for World Relief or the United Thank Offering may be obtained by writing or calling The Episcopal Church Center in New York.

# The Sundays After Pentecost

## An Overview of the Readings

During the Sundays after Pentecost, the gospel text sets the theme for the first reading and the psalm. The portions of the gospel designated for each lectionary year that have not been read during the great seasons of the church year are read in sequence; several epistles are read in sequence as well. Because both the epistles and gospels are heard in semi-continuous readings during these months, there is usually not a thematic relationship between the epistle and other lections, though the first readings and psalms are always chosen to be in thematic harmony with the gospel lection. Thus the first theme listed for each set of propers below is the theme set by the gospel text; the second theme reflects the epistle. Where only one theme is stated, all the readings for that week happen to be in thematic harmony.

The sequential reading of gospels and epistles gives a delightful opportunity to "walk through" an epistle or gospel in sermons and educational offerings. For example, in Year C, the year of reading the gospel according to Luke, Jesus is "on the road to Jerusalem" from Luke 9:51 through 13:21. In the lectionary, the "journey" portion of the gospel is read from Proper 8 (the Sunday closest to June 29) through Proper 26 (the Sunday closest to November 2). All summer we hear the gospel texts in the context of the shadow of the cross. As Jesus and the disciples draw closer to Jerusalem, the immediacy of Jesus' suffering and death is heightened. Scholars remind us that the gospel writers did not always know the context of the narratives they included in their gospels, but from Luke's perspective his "on the road" stories are to be read with the crisis of the cross increasingly in mind. Posters, banners, and bulletin covers can carry the common theme of "on the road with Jesus," week after week.

The sequential reading of several of the epistles also offers the opportunity for more indepth study of their context and overall message in the educational setting or in a serialized sermon during the liturgy. Year A, for example, provides a sixteen-week, semi-continuous reading of Romans (Proper 4 through Proper 19). As always, during these months let the lectionary establish the focus for education and liturgy.

*The Revised Common Lectionary* (published by Abingdon Press) offers alternative readings from the Hebrew scriptures during Ordinary Time that provide an interesting option for use in the educational setting. During Year A, the great stories from Genesis through the settling of the Hebrews in the promised land are heard. In Year B, stories of the great kings are heard, along with readings from the Wisdom literature of the Hebrew scriptures. Year C offers semi-continuous readings from the great literature of the prophets, highlighting the prophet Jeremiah and the stories of the eighth-century prophets Elijah and Elisha. Alternative sets of readings from the Hebrew scriptures are in thematic harmony with the gospel lections as well. These sequential readings from the Hebrew scriptures offer wonderful opportunities for summertime storytelling and education in the congregation. We can share the Bible in serialized fashion: "Come back to find out what happens next week!"

Except for Trinity Sunday, the numbered proper to be used on each of the Sundays after Pentecost is determined by the calendar date of that Sunday. Propers 1, 2, and 3 are the same as the propers for Epiphany 6, 7, and 8. When Easter falls early in the calendar, we hear these propers after Pentecost; with a late Easter, we hear them after the Feast of the Epiphany. Since Propers 1, 2, and 3 are covered in this book during the Epiphany season, we begin here with Proper 4. See page 158 of *The Book of Common Prayer* for instructions concerning the propers of the church year.

# ♦ ♦ Year A ♦ ♦

## Proper 4, Year A (The Sunday closest to June 1)

Lections: Deuteronomy 11:18-21, 26-28; Psalm 31:1-5, 19-24; Romans 3:21-25a, 28;
Matthew 7:21-27

*Theme of the lections*

The Sermon on the Mount: living by God's word must be at the center of
every Christian's life.

♦ *Epistle:* It is one's faith that brings salvation.

*Phrases for highlighting and memorization*

♦ "You shall put these words of mine in your heart and soul, and you
shall bind them as a sign on your hand, and fix them as an emblem on
your forehead." (Deut. 11:18)

♦ "Love the LORD, all you who worship him; the LORD protects the
faithful, but repays to the full those who act haughtily." (Psalm 31:23)

♦ "For we hold that a person is justified by faith apart from works
prescribed by the law." (Rom. 3:28)

♦ "Everyone then who hears these words of mine and acts on them will
be like a wise man who built his house on rock." (Matt. 7:24)

*Key words, ideas, and concepts to explore*

♦ the Sermon on the Mount;

♦ Torah;

♦ justification by faith;

♦ kingdom of heaven;

♦ This Sunday begins a sixteen-week reading of Romans. Offer an
overview of Paul's important letter.

*Christian practice and liturgical tradition*

♦ The Jewish custom of placing a symbol of God's word on the door of
the home is found in today's reading from Deuteronomy. In like
manner Christian homes are often marked with a cross or other
Christian symbol.

♦ Justification by faith (Romans 3:28) played a central role in the
Protestant Reformation.

*Formation in baptismal discipleship*
The words from Deuteronomy call us to place Christian education and
formation at the heart of congregational life.

## Proper 5, Year A (The Sunday closest to June 8)
Lections: Hosea 5:15–6:6; Psalm 50:7-15; Romans 4:13-18; Matthew 9:9-13

*Theme of the lections*
The calling of the outcasts into faithful relationship with God.
  ♦ *Epistle:* It is faith, not law, that makes one righteous before God.

*Phrases for highlighting and memorization*
  ♦ "For I desire steadfast love and not sacrifice, the knowledge of God
    rather than burnt offerings." (Hosea 6:6)
  ♦ "Offer to God a sacrifice of thanksgiving and make good your vows to
    the Most High." (Psalm 50:14)
  ♦ "For the promise that he would inherit the world did not come to
    Abraham or to his descendants through the law but through the
    righteousness of faith." (Rom. 4:13)
  ♦ "Go and learn what this means, 'I desire mercy, not sacrifice.' For I
    have come to call not the righteous but sinners." (Matt. 9:13)

*Key words, ideas, and concepts to explore*
  ♦ sacrifice and burnt offerings;
  ♦ righteousness;
  ♦ faith;
  ♦ promise;
  ♦ grace;
  ♦ sinners;
  ♦ role of the Pharisees;
  ♦ tax collectors in Jesus' time.

*Stories to tell*
  ♦ The calling of Matthew.

*Christian practice and liturgical tradition*
  ♦ A verse from today's psalm reading is often used as an offertory
    sentence at the eucharist:

*Offer to God a sacrifice of thanksgiving and make good your vows to the Most High. (Psalm 50:14)*

### Formation in baptismal discipleship
The church is called to follow Jesus' example of reaching out to those who are considered outcasts by society.

## Proper 6, Year A (The Sunday closest to June 15)
Lections: Exodus 19:2-8a; Psalm 100; Romans 5:6-11; Matthew 9:35–10:8 (9-15)

### Theme of the lections
God calls a people into intimate covenant relationship.
- *Epistle:* Christ died so that the world may know the power of God's saving love.

### Phrases for highlighting and memorization
- "But you shall be for me a priestly kingdom and a holy nation. These are the words that you shall speak to the Israelites." (Exod. 19:6)
- "Know this: The LORD himself is God; he himself has made us, and we are his; we are his people and the sheep of his pasture." (Psalm 100:2)
- "But God proves his love for us in that while we still were sinners Christ died for us." (Rom. 5:8)
- "Then Jesus summoned his twelve disciples and gave them authority over unclean spirits, to cast them out, and to cure every disease and every sickness." (Matt. 10:1)

### Key words, ideas, and concepts to explore
- kingdom of priests;
- apostolic authority;
- disciples;
- Christ's sacrificial death for sinners;
- sheep and shepherds;
- names of the disciples (gospel accounts show some variations).

### Stories to tell
- The making of the covenant at Mt. Sinai.

### Christian practice and liturgical tradition
- Bishops receive and pass on the apostolic authority of the disciples.
- The Baptismal Covenant (BCP 304-305) reflects the ancient covenant made with Israel at Mt. Sinai.

### Formation in baptismal discipleship
The Baptismal Covenant becomes the focus for life in the church. The church can measure its faithfulness to the gospel by setting the life of the congregation alongside the provisions of the covenant.


## Proper 7, Year A (The Sunday closest to June 22)
Lections: Jeremiah 20:7-13; Psalm 69:7-10, 16-18; Romans 5:15b-19; Matthew 10:(16-23) 24-33

### Theme of the lections
The cost of discipleship.
- *Epistle:* Jesus' obedience overcomes human alienation represented by Adam.

### Phrases for highlighting and memorization
- "For whenever I speak, I must cry out, I must shout, 'Violence and destruction!'" (Jer. 20:8a)
- "Surely, for your sake have I suffered reproach, and shame has covered my face." (Psalm 69:8)
- "For just as by the one man's disobedience the many were made sinners, so by the one man's obedience the many will be made righteous." (Rom. 5:19)
- "Everyone therefore who acknowledges me before others, I also will acknowledge before my Father in heaven." (Matt. 10:32)

### Key words, ideas, and concepts to explore
- righteousness;
- grace;
- trespass;
- Adam;
- role of the prophet in the Old Testament;
- witness;
- radical nature of discipleship.

### Christian practice and liturgical tradition

- The sentences the bishop says at the time of confirmation speak of the cost of taking up the role of disciple in the world today:

  *Strengthen, O Lord, your servant N. with your Holy Spirit; empower* him *for your service; and sustain* him *all the days of* his *life....Defend, O Lord, your servant N. with your heavenly grace, that* he *may continue yours for ever....* (BCP 309)

### Formation in baptismal discipleship

The church must witness to the radical call of the gospel, which often means a conflict with family members and even secular authority.


## Proper 8, Year A (The Sunday closest to June 29)

Lections: Isaiah 2:10-17; Psalm 89:1-4, 15-18; Romans 6:3-11; Matthew 10:34-42

### Theme of the lections

The cost of discipleship.

- *Epistle:* Alive in Christ through baptism.

### Phrases for highlighting and memorization

- "The haughtiness of people shall be humbled, and the pride of everyone shall be brought low; and the LORD alone will be exalted on that day." (Isa. 2:17)
- "Righteousness and justice are the foundations of your throne; love and truth go before your face." (Psalm 89:14)
- "But if we have died with Christ, we believe that we will also live with him." (Rom. 6:8)
- "Those who find their life will lose it, and those who lose their life for my sake will find it." (Matt. 10:39)

### Key words, ideas, and concepts to explore

- discipleship;
- baptism;
- newness of life;
- enslaved to sin;
- resurrection.

### Christian practice and liturgical tradition

◆ The traditions associated with Holy Week come from the early church. With Paul's words in mind, candidates for baptism were led through an experience of participating in the death of Jesus so that they could participate in his resurrection.

### Formation in baptismal discipleship

The congregation must enter into the struggle for justice that comes from proclaiming the gospel to an often hostile world.

## Proper 9, Year A (The Sunday closest to July 6)

Lections: Zechariah 9:9-12; Psalm 145:8-14; Romans 7:21–8:6; Matthew 11:25-30

### Theme of the lections

God's wisdom, which brings rest and peace, is personified in Jesus.

◆ *Epistle:* Christ overcomes the struggle against sin and evil.

### Phrases for highlighting and memorization

◆ "Lo, your king comes to you; triumphant and victorious is he, humble and riding on a donkey, on a colt, the foal of a donkey....He shall command peace to the nations; his dominion shall be from sea to sea, and from the River to the ends of the earth." (Zech. 9:9-10)

◆ "The LORD is faithful in all his words and merciful in all his deeds." (Psalm 145:14)

◆ "For the law of the Spirit of life in Christ Jesus has set you free from the law of sin and of death." (Rom. 8:2)

◆ "Come to me, all you that are weary and are carrying heavy burdens, and I will give you rest." (Matt. 11:28)

### Key words, ideas, and concepts to explore

◆ God's wisdom (revealed through Jesus);
◆ the reign (or kingdom) of God;
◆ God's gift of rest;
◆ evil;
◆ law of God;
◆ deliverance through Jesus Christ.

*Christian practice and liturgical tradition*
- ◆ The Zechariah text lies behind Jesus' triumphant entry into Jerusalem and the traditions of Palm Sunday.

*Formation in baptismal discipleship*
The church is called to witness to the wisdom of God, which often contradicts the "wisdom" of the culture. The church is to proclaim the way of God's wisdom and peace in its every action and word.


## Proper 10, Year A (The Sunday closest to July 13)
Lections: Isaiah 55:1-5, 10-13; Psalm 65:9-14; Romans 8:9-17; Matthew 13:1-9, 18-23

*Theme of the lections*
God's word is power (the parable of the sower).
- ◆ *Epistle:* We are children and heirs of God.

*Phrases for highlighting and memorization*
- ◆ "So shall my word be that goes out from my mouth; it shall not return to me empty, but it shall accomplish that which I purpose, and succeed in the thing for which I sent it." (Isa. 55:11)
- ◆ "You prepare the grain, for so you provide for the earth." (Psalm 65:10)
- ◆ "When we cry, 'Abba! Father!' it is that very Spirit bearing witness with our spirit that we are children of God." (Rom. 8:15b-16)
- ◆ "And he told them many things in parables." (Matt. 13:3a)

*Key words, ideas, and concepts to explore*
- ◆ parable;
- ◆ planting and reaping;
- ◆ God's word;
- ◆ living in the Spirit.

*Stories to tell*
- ◆ The parable of the sower.

### Christian practice and liturgical tradition

> ◆ Paul's description of living in the Spirit is conveyed in the anointing at baptism: "You are sealed by the Holy Spirit in Baptism and marked as Christ's own forever" (BCP 308).

### Formation in baptismal discipleship

The church must challenge the assumptions of society. The power of story and drama is seen as a tool of prophetic witness.

## Proper 11, Year A (The Sunday closest to July 20)

Lections: Wisdom 12:13, 16-19; Psalm 86:11-17; Romans 8:18-25; Matthew 13:24-30, 36-43

### Theme of the lections

God's patience and mercy.

> ◆ *Epistle:* God's glory surpasses the suffering of the present moment.

### Phrases for highlighting and memorization

> ◆ "Although you are sovereign in strength, you judge with mildness, and with great forbearance you govern us; for you have power to act whenever you choose." (Wis. 12:18)
> ◆ "For great is your love toward me; you have delivered me from the nethermost Pit." (Psalm 86:13)
> ◆ "I consider that the sufferings of this present time are not worth comparing with the glory about to be revealed to us." (Rom. 8:18)
> ◆ "Let anyone with ears listen!" (Matt. 13:43b)

### Key words, ideas, and concepts to explore

> ◆ parable;
> ◆ judgment;
> ◆ mercy;
> ◆ glory to be revealed;
> ◆ hope.

### Stories to tell

> ◆ The parable of weeds among the wheat.

### Christian practice and liturgical tradition

♦ This section of Romans is often read at a burial service because it expresses with power the Christian hope.

### Formation in baptismal discipleship

The church must reflect God's patience and avoid passing judgment on others.

## Proper 12, Year A (The Sunday closest to July 27)

Lections: 1 Kings 3:5-12; Psalm 119:129-136; Romans 8:26-34; Matthew 13:31-33, 44-49a

### Theme of the lections

The hidden power of the kingdom of God.

♦ *Epistle:* The work of the Spirit in prayer. The relationship between God and those God calls.

### Phrases for highlighting and memorization

♦ "Give your servant therefore an understanding mind to govern your people, able to discern between good and evil; for who can govern this your great people?" (1 Kings 3:9)
♦ "When your word goes forth it gives light; it gives understanding to the simple." (Psalm 119:130)
♦ "We know that all things work together for good for those who love God, who are called according to his purpose." (Rom. 8:28)
♦ "The kingdom of heaven is like treasure hidden in a field, which someone found and hid; then in his joy he goes and sells all that he has and buys that field." (Matt. 13:44)

### Key words, ideas, and concepts to explore

♦ discernment;
♦ Solomon;
♦ intercession;
♦ predestined;
♦ justification;
♦ mustard seeds;
♦ kingdom of heaven.

### Stories to tell

* The story of Solomon's prayer for God's wisdom.

### Formation in baptismal discipleship

The epistle reading points to the dynamic role of the Holy Spirit in the life of the individual and the church.

## Proper 13, Year A (The Sunday closest to August 3)

Lections: Nehemiah 9:16-20; Psalm 78:14-20, 23-25; Romans 8:35-39; Matthew 14:13-21

### Theme of the lections

Jesus' compassion for the people leads him to respond with food for mind and body. The feeding of the five thousand expresses the significance of the Holy Eucharist.

* *Epistle:* Nothing can separate us from the love of Christ.

### Phrases for highlighting and memorization

* "You are a God ready to forgive, gracious and merciful, slow to anger and abounding in steadfast love." (Neh. 9:17b)
* "He rained down manna upon them to eat and gave them grain from heaven." (Psalm 78:24)
* "For I am convinced that neither death, nor life, nor angels, nor rulers, nor things present, nor things to come, nor powers, nor height, nor depth, nor anything else in all creation, will be able to separate us from the love of God in Christ Jesus our Lord." (Rom. 8:38-39)
* "And all ate and were filled; and they took up what was left over of the broken pieces, twelve baskets full." (Matt. 14:20)

### Key words, ideas, and concepts to explore

* bread (manna);
* eucharistic actions (took bread, blessed, broke, gave);
* blood of Christ;
* reconciliation;
* steadfast love.

### Stories to tell

* The feeding of the five thousand.

### Christian practice and liturgical tradition

- There are eucharistic overtones to this day's gospel story. Jesus "took bread, blessed the bread, broke it, and distributed it among the people." Notice that Jesus "feeds" the people first with teaching and then with bread. At the eucharist we first hear the word and then receive the eucharistic bread: word and sacrament lie at the heart of Christian life.
- The epistle text is listed in *The Book of Common Prayer* as an option for use at burials because it is an eloquent statement of Christian hope.

### Formation in baptismal discipleship

Christ has compassion for the people of the church and the world that hunger for God's word.


## Proper 14, Year A (The Sunday closest to August 10)

Lections: Jonah 2:1-9; Psalm 29; Romans 9:1-5; Matthew 14:22-33

### Theme of the lections

God's power is revealed as Jesus controls the waters.

- *Epistle:* Paul mourns for the Israelites, who are the true foundation for the coming of the Messiah.

### Phrases for highlighting and memorization

- "Deliverance belongs to the LORD!" (Jonah 2:9b)
- "The voice of the LORD is upon the waters; the God of glory thunders; the LORD is upon the mighty waters." (Psalm 29:3)
- "I have great sorrow and unceasing anguish in my heart. For I could wish that I myself were accursed and cut off from Christ for the sake of my own people, my kindred according to the flesh." (Rom. 9:2-3)
- "But when the disciples saw him walking on the sea, they were terrified, saying, 'It is a ghost!' And they cried out in fear. But immediately Jesus spoke to them and said, 'Take heart, it is I; do not be afraid.'" (Matt. 14:26-27)

### Key words, ideas, and concepts to explore

- Jonah;
- God's power over the waters (first expressed in Genesis 1).

### Stories to tell

- Jesus walking on the water;
- Jonah (the power of God to save Jonah from the sea is incidental to the book's purpose, however).

### Christian practice and liturgical tradition

- The Thanksgiving over the Water in the baptismal rite emphasizes the times in salvation history when God's power and calling were revealed through the waters.

### Formation in baptismal discipleship

We come to the new life of God in Christ through the waters of baptism.


## Proper 15, Year A (The Sunday closest to August 17)

Lections: Isaiah 56:1(2-5)6-7; Psalm 67; Romans 11:13-15, 29-32; Matthew 15:21-28

### Theme of the lections

Faith brings salvation to Jews and Gentiles alike.

### Phrases for highlighting and memorization

- "My house shall be called a house of prayer for all peoples." (Isa. 56:7c)
- "Let your ways be known upon earth, your saving health among all nations." (Psalm 67:2)
- "The gifts and the calling of God are irrevocable." (Rom. 11:29)
- "Then Jesus answered her, 'Woman, great is your faith! Let it be done for you as you wish.' And her daughter was healed instantly." (Matt. 15:28)

### Key words, ideas, and concepts to explore

- covenant;
- God's holy mountain;
- burnt offerings and sacrifices;
- Gentiles;
- evangelizing society's outcasts.

### Formation in baptismal discipleship

The congregation is called to live for others so that all may know the power of God's salvation revealed through Christ. Evangelism is the means by which the church proclaims the good news of salvation to all peoples.

## Proper 16, Year A (The Sunday closest to August 24)

Lections: Isaiah 51:1-6; Psalm 138; Romans 11:33-36; Matthew 16:13-20

### Theme of the lections

The foundation of faith.
- *Epistle:* God's knowledge has been revealed through Jesus.

### Phrases for highlighting and memorization

- "But my salvation will be forever, and my deliverance will never be ended." (Isa. 51:6c)
- "Though I walk in the midst of trouble, you keep me safe; you stretch forth your hand against the fury of my enemies; your right hand shall save me." (Psalm 138:8)
- "O the depth of the riches and wisdom and knowledge of God! How unsearchable are his judgments and how inscrutable his ways!" (Rom. 11:33)
- "And I tell you, you are Peter, and on this rock I will build my church, and the gates of Hades will not prevail against it." (Matt. 16:18)

### Key words, ideas, and concepts to explore

- salvation;
- deliverance;
- Peter as "the rock" ("Peter" means "rock" in Greek).

### Christian practice and liturgical tradition

- The gospel text establishes a sense of authority for the role of the bishop in the church. As Jesus had authority to act for God in the world, so the church has authority to "bind and loose," and its bishops are seen as symbols of that apostolic authority in the church today. In the Roman Catholic tradition, the gospel text is cited as the authority for the primacy of the Bishop of Rome (the Pope).

## Proper 17, Year A (The Sunday closest to August 31)

Lections: Jeremiah 15:15-21; Psalm 26:1-8; Romans 12:1-8; Matthew 16:21-27

### Theme of the lections
The cost of discipleship.

### Phrases for highlighting and memorization

* "In your forbearance do not take me away; know that on your account I suffer insult." (Jer. 15:15b)
* "Give judgment for me, O LORD, for I have lived with integrity; I have trusted in the Lord and have not faltered." (Psalm 26:1)
* "I appeal to you therefore, brothers and sisters, by the mercies of God, to present your bodies as a living sacrifice, holy and acceptable to God, which is your spiritual worship." (Rom. 12:1)
* "Then Jesus told his disciples, 'If any want to become my followers, let them deny themselves and take up their cross and follow me.'" (Matt. 16:24)

### Key words, ideas, and concepts to explore

* discipleship;
* sacrifice;
* sacrificial offerings set forth in the Torah;
* transformation;
* gifts of the Spirit;
* Body of Christ;
* taking up the cross.

### Christian practice and liturgical tradition

* The services of Holy Week provide a symbolic way of walking in the way of the cross.
* The offertory at the Holy Eucharist is to express the offering of our lives to God.
* A phrase from Eucharistic Prayer 1 reflects Paul's words heard in the second reading:

  *And here we offer and present unto thee, O Lord, our selves, our souls and bodies, to be a reasonable, holy, and living sacrifice unto thee.* (BCP 336)

### Formation in baptismal discipleship
The church remembers and honors saints and martyrs who have borne the cost of discipleship.


## Proper 18, Year A (The Sunday closest to September 7)
Lections: Ezekiel 33:(1-6)7-11; Psalm 119:33-40; Romans 12:9-21; Matthew 18:15-20

### Theme of the lections
The church is vested with Jesus' authority. Guidelines for discipline and other aspects of church life.

### Phrases for highlighting and memorization
- "Say to them, As I live, says the Lord GOD, I have no pleasure in the death of the wicked, but that the wicked turn from their ways and live." (Ezek. 33:11a)
- "Turn away the reproach which I dread, because your judgments are good." (Psalm 119:39)
- "Rejoice with those who rejoice, weep with those who weep." (Rom. 12:15)
- "For where two or three are gathered in my name, I am there among them." (Matt. 18:20)

### Key words, ideas, and concepts to explore
- discipline;
- excommunication;
- forgiveness;
- judgment;
- repentance.

### Christian practice and liturgical tradition
- The Disciplinary Rubrics set forth guidelines for church discipline based on the gospel lection (BCP 409).

### Formation in baptismal discipleship
People are truly formed as Christians when they are part of a congregation that lives out Paul's words, "Rejoice with those who rejoice, weep with those who weep."

# Proper 19, Year A (The Sunday closest to September 14)

Lections: Ecclesiasticus 27:30–28:7; Psalm 103:8-13; Romans 14:5-12; Matthew 18:21-35

### Theme of the lections
"Forgive us our sins as we forgive those who have sinned against us."

### Phrases for highlighting and memorization
- "Forgive your neighbor the wrong he has done, and then your sins will be pardoned when you pray." (Ecclesiasticus 28:2)
- "He has not dealt with us according to our sins, nor rewarded us according to our wickedness." (Psalm 103:10)
- "Why do you pass judgment on your brother or sister? Or you, why do you despise your brother or sister? For we will all stand before the judgment seat of God." (Rom. 14:10)
- "Jesus said to him, 'Not seven times, but, I tell you, seventy-seven times.'" (Matt. 18:22)

### Key words, ideas, and concepts to explore
- forgiveness;
- sins;
- judgment.

### Stories to tell
- The parable of the unforgiving servant.

### Christian practice and liturgical tradition
- The Lord's Prayer reflects the parable and Jesus' admonition. Each time we gather for worship we pray that we will be forgiven to the extent that we are ready to forgive others.
- The passing of the peace is an acting out of this forgiveness principle. God's forgiveness must be passed on to others if it is to be realized in our own lives.

    *So when you are offering your gift at the altar, if you remember that your brother or sister has something against you, leave your gift there before the altar and go; first be reconciled to your brother or sister, and then come and offer your gift. (Matt. 5:23-24)*

### Formation in baptismal discipleship
Congregational life must express the forgiveness found in today's texts, including the healing of divisions within the congregation.


## Proper 20, Year A (The Sunday closest to September 21)
Lections: Jonah 3:10–4:11; Psalm 145:1-8; Philippians 1:21-27; Matthew 20:1-16

### Theme of the lections
God's gracious compassion for all people extends beyond human understanding.
- *Epistle:* Paul's desire to be with Christ must be put aside in order that he may be with the church.

### Phrases for highlighting and memorization
- "And should I not be concerned about Nineveh, that great city, in which there are more than a hundred and twenty thousand persons who do not know their right hand from their left, and also many animals?" (Jonah 4:11)
- "The LORD is gracious and full of compassion, slow to anger and of great kindness." (Psalm 145:8)
- "For to me, living is Christ and dying is gain." (Phil. 1:21)
- "Am I not allowed to do what I choose with what belongs to me? Or are you envious because I am generous?" (Matt. 20:15)

### Key words, ideas, and concepts to explore
- God's boundless grace and compassion;
- the nature of parables;
- "to live is Christ";
- This Sunday begins four-week, semi-continuous reading of Philippians. Take time to introduce this epistle.

### Stories to tell
- The parable of the laborers in the vineyard;
- The story of Jonah, Nineveh, and the shade plant.

### Formation in baptismal discipleship
The church is called to reach out to the very people who are neglected and despised by society.

## Proper 21, Year A (The Sunday closest to September 28)

Lections: Ezekiel 18:1-4, 25-32; Psalm 25:3-9; Philippians 2:1-13; Matthew 21:28-32

### Theme of the lections

Society's outcasts are often more righteous before God than those who consider themselves righteous.

- *Epistle:* God came in Jesus Christ to become servant to the world even to the point of death.

### Phrases for highlighting and memorization

- "When the righteous turn away from their righteousness and commit iniquity, they shall die for it; for the iniquity that they have committed they shall die. Again, when the wicked turn away from the wickedness they have committed and do what is lawful and right, they shall save their life." (Ezek. 18:26-27)
- "All the paths of the LORD are love and faithfulness to those who keep his covenant and his testimonies." (Psalm 25:9)
- "Let the same mind be in you that was in Christ Jesus." (Phil. 2:5)
- "Truly I tell you, the tax collectors and the prostitutes are going into the kingdom of God ahead of you." (Matt. 21:31b)

### Key words, ideas, and concepts to explore

- Christ as God, yet servant;
- true righteousness;
- repentance;
- wickedness.

### Stories to tell

- The parable of the two sons.

### Christian practice and liturgical tradition

- The season of Lent points to the need to turn back to God's way.
- Philippians 2:6-11 may have been one of the church's earliest hymns.

### Formation in baptismal discipleship

Christians are called to take on the mind of Christ, full of humility and love for others, and to follow paths of faithfulness.

# Proper 22, Year A (The Sunday closest to October 5)

Lections: Isaiah 5:1-7; Psalm 80:7-14; Philippians 3:14-21; Matthew 21:33-43

### Theme of the lections

In the parable of the vineyard, Isaiah and Jesus both warn God's people that they will be held accountable for the fruits of the covenant.

- *Epistle:* The Christian must concentrate on God's coming reign and not on the present age.

### Phrases for highlighting and memorization

- "For the vineyard of the LORD of hosts is the house of Israel, and the people of Judah are his pleasant planting; he expected justice, but saw bloodshed; righteousness, but heard a cry!" (Isa. 5:7)
- "You have brought a vine out of Egypt; you cast out the nations and planted it." (Psalm 80:8)
- "I press on toward the goal for the prize of the heavenly call of God in Christ Jesus." (Phil. 3:14)
- "Therefore I tell you, the kingdom of God will be taken away from you and given to a people that produces the fruits of the kingdom." (Matt. 21:43)

### Key words, ideas, and concepts to explore

- stewardship;
- fruits of the kingdom;
- judgment.

### Stories to tell

- The parable of the wicked tenants.

### Christian practice and liturgical tradition

- The Baptismal Covenant provides a way of assessing the church's stewardship of God's vineyard.

### Formation in baptismal discipleship

Stewardship is more than a financial pledge to the church. It is a way of life in which we all recognize our responsibility to be faithful stewards.

## Proper 23, Year A (The Sunday closest to October 12)

Lections: Isaiah 25:1-9; Psalm 23; Philippians 4:4-13; Matthew 22:1-14

### Theme of the lections

God's coming reign will be like a great banquet (often referred to as the "messianic banquet"), but we must be ready to accept the invitation.

 ◆ *Epistle:* Live with joy in God's peace.

### Phrases for highlighting and memorization

 ◆ "On this mountain the LORD of hosts will make for all peoples a feast of rich food, a feast of well-aged wines, of rich food filled with marrow, of well-aged wines strained clear." (Isa. 25:6)
 ◆ "You spread a table before me in the presence of those who trouble me; you have anointed my head with oil, and my cup is running over." (Psalm 23:5)
 ◆ "And the peace of God, which surpasses all understanding, will guard your hearts and your minds in Christ Jesus." (Phil. 4:7)
 ◆ "Go therefore into the main streets, and invite everyone you find to the wedding banquet." (Matt. 22:9)

### Key words, ideas, and concepts to explore

 ◆ peace of God;
 ◆ messianic banquet;
 ◆ hospitality in the early church;
 ◆ kingdom of heaven (or reign of God).

### Stories to tell

 ◆ The parable of the banquet. (The simpler version of this parable is found in Luke 14:16-24; the story of the guest without a proper garment is a separate parable that was added by the writer of Matthew.)

### Christian practice and liturgical tradition

 ◆ It is often said that the Holy Eucharist is a foretaste of the "messianic banquet." Jesus may have been referring to this coming banquet when he said, "For I tell you that from now on I will not drink of the fruit of the vine until the kingdom of God comes" (Luke 22:18).

### Formation in baptismal discipleship
Christians extend the invitation to the banquet in their regular participation in worship and in their involvement in congregational ministry and life.


## Proper 24, Year A (The Sunday closest to October 19)
Lections: Isaiah 45:1-7; Psalm 96:1-9; 1 Thessalonians 1:1-10; Matthew 22:15-22

### Theme of the lections
God's power and will can be revealed even among those considered enemies or aliens. Since God's power extends to everyone, ultimate authority belongs to God.
  - *Epistle:* Paul greets the church at Thessalonica with praise for their witness and support.

### Phrases for highlighting and memorization
  - "Thus says the LORD to his anointed, to Cyrus, whose right hand I have grasped to subdue nations before him and strip kings of their robes, to open doors before him—and the gates shall not be closed." (Isa. 45:1)
  - "Declare his glory among the nations and his wonders among all peoples." (Psalm 96:3)
  - "Our message of the gospel came to you not in word only, but also in power and in the Holy Spirit and with full conviction. (1 Thess. 1:5b)
  - "Give therefore to the emperor the things that are the emperor's, and to God the things that are God's." (Matt. 22:21b)

### Key words, ideas, and concepts to explore
  - the role of Cyrus of Persia as God's anointed;
  - the authority of Caesar over Judea in Jesus' time;
  - This Sunday begins a five-week, semi-continuous reading of 1 Thessalonians, in which Paul deals with the "endtimes." Take time to introduce the letter and the theology behind it.

### Christian practice and liturgical tradition
  - The rubrics for the Prayers of the People specify that the gathered church must pray for "the Nation and all in authority," and "the welfare of the world" at every celebration of the eucharist (BCP 383).

### Formation in baptismal discipleship

The church must acknowledge the ultimate allegiance to God. It is important for the congregation to know the stories of those who have witnessed to that ultimate authority with their lives. Dietrich Bonhoeffer, a German theologian killed by the Nazi regime, is an example of the witnesses we have in Christian history.

## Proper 25, Year A (The Sunday closest to October 26)

Lections: Exodus 22:21-27; Psalm 1; 1 Thessalonians 2:1-8; Matthew 22:34-46

### Theme of the lections

To be righteous before God means doing right to the neighbor, the sojourner, and the person in need. To love God is to love the neighbor.

- *Epistle:* Paul reminds the church in Thessalonica of the relationship he established with them when he was in their midst.

### Phrases for highlighting and memorization

- "You shall not wrong or oppress a resident alien, for you were aliens in the land of Egypt." (Exod. 22:21)
- "Their delight is in the law of the LORD, and they meditate on his law day and night." (Psalm 1:2)
- "So deeply do we care for you that we are determined to share with you not only the gospel of God but also our own selves, because you have become very dear to us." (1 Thess. 2:8)
- "He said to him, '"You shall love the Lord your God with all your heart, and with all your soul, and with all your mind." This is the greatest and first commandment. And a second is like it: "You shall love your neighbor as yourself." On these two commandments hang all the law and the prophets.'" (Matt. 22:37-40)

### Key words, ideas, and concepts to explore

- commandments;
- the law of the Lord;
- the Shema;
- God's compassion for the poor;
- loving our neighbors as ourselves.

### Christian practice and liturgical tradition
♦ The Baptismal Covenant repeats the commandments to love God and neighbor.

### Formation in baptismal discipleship
To embody the covenant means responding to God in praise, seeking and serving Christ in others, and striving for justice and peace (BCP 305).

## Proper 26, Year A (The Sunday closest to November 2)
Lections: Micah 3:5-12; Psalm 43; 1 Thessalonians 2:9-13, 17-20, Matthew 23:1-12

### Theme of the lections
Those in authority must not mislead the people. They must practice what they preach.
♦ *Epistle:* Paul reflects on his life with the Thessalonians.

### Phrases for highlighting and memorization
♦ "Its rulers give judgment for a bribe, its priests teach for a price, its prophets give oracles for money; yet they lean upon the LORD and say, 'Surely the LORD is with us! No harm shall come upon us.'" (Micah 3:11)
♦ "Send out your light and your truth, that they may lead me, and bring me to your holy hill and to your dwelling." (Psalm 43:3)
♦ "We also constantly give thanks to God for this, that when you received the word of God that you heard from us, you accepted it not as a human word but as what it really is, God's word, which is also at work in you believers." (1 Thess. 2:13)
♦ "The scribes and the Pharisees sit on Moses' seat; therefore, do whatever they teach you and follow it; but do not do as they do, for they do not practice what they teach." (Matt. 23:2-3)

### Key words, ideas, and concepts to explore
♦ scribes and Pharisees;
♦ humility;
♦ false prophets;
♦ injustice;
♦ ordination.

### Christian practice and liturgical tradition

◆ Ordination and baptismal rites reflect the call to humility and servanthood, hallmarks of the Christian life.

### Formation in baptismal discipleship

All the ministries of the church are to model the humble servant ministry of Jesus: "The greatest among you will be your servant. All who exalt themselves will be humbled, and all who humble themselves will be exalted" (Matt. 23:11-12).

## Proper 27, Year A (The Sunday closest to November 9)

Lections: Amos 5:18-24; Psalm 70; 1 Thessalonians 4:13-18; Matthew 25:1-13

### Theme of the lections

Being ready for judgment means striving for justice and righteousness.

(Note: The themes of the season of Advent begin to be expressed this week, offering an opportunity to explore the rich heritage of Advent. All three readings focus on the coming of Christ in glory and on the last judgment.)

◆ *Epistle:* Both the living and the dead will be united in Christ at the Lord's coming.

### Phrases for highlighting and memorization

◆ "Take away from me the noise of your songs; I will not listen to the melody of your harps. But let justice roll down like waters, and righteousness like an everflowing stream." (Amos 5:23-24)
◆ "You are my helper and my deliverer; O LORD, do not tarry." (Psalm 70:6)
◆ "Then we who are alive, who are left, will be caught up in the clouds together with them to meet the Lord in the air; and so we will be with the Lord forever." (1 Thess. 4:17)
◆ "Keep awake therefore, for you know neither the day nor the hour." (Matt. 25:13)

### Key words, ideas, and concepts to explore

◆ the coming of the Lord;
◆ judgment day;
◆ justice;

- empty worship practices;
- parable.

### Stories to tell
- The parable of the ten bridesmaids.

### Christian practice and liturgical tradition
- The Apostles' Creed and the Nicene Creed affirm the resurrection of the dead and the final judgment: "He will come again in glory to judge the living and the dead, and his kingdom will have no end" (BCP 359).
- "The Christian Hope" section of An Outline of the Faith (BCP 861-862) discusses the final things.
- The joy of the resurrection is reflected in the traditions of Christian burial. See the rubric that begins, "The liturgy for the dead is an Easter liturgy. It finds all its meaning in the resurrection. Because Jesus was raised from the dead, we, too, shall be raised" (BCP 507).

### Formation in baptismal discipleship
The congregation lives in the light of the resurrection and the final judgment. Hope and judgment characterize the outlook of the church as it proclaims Christ to the world.


## Proper 28, Year A (The Sunday closest to November 16)
Lections: Zephaniah 1:7, 12-18; Psalm 90:1-8, 12; 1 Thessalonians 5:1-10; Matthew 25:14-15, 19-29

### Theme of the lections
Being ready for the final judgment.

### Phrases for highlighting and memorization
- "At that time I will search Jerusalem with lamps, and I will punish the people who rest complacently on their dregs, those who say in their hearts, 'The LORD will not do good, nor will he do harm.'" (Zeph. 1:12)
- "Who regards the power of your wrath? who rightly fears your indignation?" (Psalm 90:11)
- "For you yourselves know very well that the day of the Lord will come like a thief in the night." (1 Thess. 5:2)

- "After a long time the master of those slaves came and settled accounts with them." (Matt. 25:19)

### Key words, ideas, and concepts to explore
- the day of the Lord;
- judgment day;
- wrath;
- justice.

### Stories to tell
- The parable of the talents.

### Christian practice and liturgical tradition
See Proper 27, Year A, and general remarks in the chapter concerning the season of Advent.

### Formation in baptismal discipleship
See Proper 27, Year A, and general remarks in the chapter concerning the season of Advent.


## Proper 29, Year A (The Sunday closest to November 23)
Lections: Ezekiel 34:11-17; Psalm 95:1-7; 1 Corinthians 15:20-28; Matthew 25:31-46

### Theme of the lections
This day is often referred to as the Sunday of Christ the King, or The Reign of Christ. Christ's sovereignty is the major theme in the lections for all three years.

### Phrases for highlighting and memorization
- "I will seek the lost, and I will bring back the strayed, and I will bind up the injured, and I will strengthen the weak, but the fat and the strong I will destroy. I will feed them with justice." (Ezek. 34:16)
- "For he is our God, and we are the people of his pasture and the sheep of his hand. Oh, that today you would hearken to his voice!" (Psalm 95:7)
- "Then comes the end, when he hands over the kingdom to God the Father, after he has destroyed every ruler and every authority and power." (1 Cor. 15:24)

- "And the king will answer them, 'Truly I tell you, just as you did it to one of the least of these who are members of my family, you did it to me.'" (Matt. 25:40)

### Key words, ideas, and concepts to explore
- Christ as king or sovereign;
- kingdom of God;
- the work of a shepherd.

### Stories to tell
- The story of the king sitting in judgment from Matthew.

### Christian practice and liturgical tradition
- Some of the traditions associated with worship in the Episcopal Church have their origins in the royal court: for example, purple, the color for Advent and Lent, was the color associated with royalty and became linked to the coming of Christ as king.
- The psalms and prayers of the church are filled with imagery of the ruler.

### Formation in baptismal discipleship
"Jesus is Lord" (the earliest Christian creed) means that Jesus stands above all other earthly power and authority. All through history and into the present moment, choosing God above earthly authority has caused persecution and conflict in the life of the church. The congregation and wider church must witness always to the authority of Jesus Christ, realizing that there will be times when conflict will be the direct result of such a witness.

## Proper 4, Year B (The Sunday closest to June 1)

Lections: Deuteronomy 5:6-21; Psalm 81:1-10; 2 Corinthians 4:5-12; Mark 2:23-28

### Theme of the lections
Jesus has ultimate authority, even over the commandments of the Torah.
- *Epistle:* For Paul, participating in Christ's death means living in a way that Jesus' presence is experienced in the lives of the faithful.

### Phrases for highlighting and memorization
- "You shall have no other gods before me." (Deut. 5:7)
- "I am the LORD your God, who brought you out of the land of Egypt and said, 'Open your mouth wide, and I will fill it.'" (Psalm 81:10)
- "For while we live, we are always being given up to death for Jesus' sake, so that the life of Jesus may be made visible in our mortal flesh." (2 Cor. 4:11)
- "The sabbath was made for humankind, and not humankind for the sabbath; so the Son of Man is lord even of the sabbath." (Mark 2:27b-28)

### Key words, ideas, and concepts to explore
- Ten Commandments;
- Torah;
- Sabbath;
- ultimate authority of Jesus;
- treasure in earthen vessels;
- bearing the cross of Christ;
- This week begins a six-week reading of 2 Corinthians. Take time in the educational setting to provide an overview of the epistle.

### Christian practice and liturgical tradition
- Discuss the origin of the Ten Commandments, memorized by generations of Jewish and Christian children. (See also Exodus 20:1-21.)
- The Ten Commandments play an important role in A Penitential Order (BCP 317-321/350-353).

**Formation in baptismal discipleship**

The sense of covenant that incorporates demands for faithfulness with the promise of abundant life lies at the heart of Christian life; at the same time, the church lives by grace and not by law.


## Proper 5, Year B (The Sunday closest to June 8)

Lections: Genesis 3:(1-7) 8-21; Psalm 130; 2 Corinthians 4:13-18; Mark 3:20-35

### Theme of the lections

Doing the will of God.

- *Epistle:* Faith leads to hope even in the face of adversity.

### Phrases for highlighting and memorization

- "But the LORD God called to the man, and said to him, 'Where are you?'" (Gen. 3:9)
- "If you, LORD, were to note what is done amiss, O Lord, who could stand?" (Psalm 130:2)
- "We also believe, and so we speak, because we know that the one who raised the Lord Jesus will raise us also with Jesus, and will bring us with you into his presence." (2 Cor. 4:13b-14)
- "Whoever does the will of God is my brother and sister and mother." (Mark 3:35)

### Key words, ideas, and concepts to explore

- disobedience;
- hubris (wanting to be like God);
- faith;
- thanksgiving;
- Satan;
- Beelzebub;
- demons;
- being brothers and sisters of Christ.

### Stories to tell

- The story of Adam and Eve.

### Christian practice and liturgical tradition
- Ash Wednesday liturgy: "Remember that you are dust, and to dust you shall return" (BCP 265).
- The Burial of the Dead: "We commit *his* body to the ground; earth to earth, ashes to ashes, dust to dust" (BCP 501).

### Formation in baptismal discipleship
An awareness of the need for humility in the face of God's ultimate wisdom and authority must inform the life of the congregation and the individual Christian.


## Proper 6, Year B (The Sunday closest to June 15)
Lections: Ezekiel 31:1-6, 10-14; Psalm 92:1-4, 11-14; 2 Corinthians 5:1-10; Mark 4:26-34

### Theme of the lections
The kingdom of God arrives through God's grace, not by human striving for power.
- *Epistle:* Paul realizes that his real destiny is yet to come.

### Phrases for highlighting and memorization
- "All the birds of the air made their nests in its boughs; under its branches all the animals of the field gave birth to their young; and in its shade all great nations lived." (Ezek. 31:6)
- "The righteous shall flourish like a palm tree, and shall spread abroad like a cedar of Lebanon." (Psalm 92:11)
- "For we know that if the earthly tent we live in is destroyed, we have a building from God, a house not made with hands, eternal in the heavens." (2 Cor. 5:1)
- "Yet when it is sown it grows up and becomes the greatest of all shrubs, and puts forth large branches, so that the birds of the air can make nests in its shade." (Mark 4:32)

### Key words, ideas, and concepts to explore
- kingdom of God;
- parable;
- the mustard plant;
- harvest;
- hubris.

### Stories to tell

* The parables of the growing seed and mustard seed.

### Christian practice and liturgical tradition

* The traditions associated with Rogation Days emphasize God's presence in the mystery of creation and growth in the natural world. The proper for Rogation Days I includes the text from today's gospel (BCP 930).

## Proper 7, Year B (The Sunday closest to June 22)

Lections: Job 38:1-11, 16-18; Psalm 107:1-3, 23-32; 2 Corinthians 5:14-21; Mark 4:35-41 (5:1-20)

### Theme of the lections

God's power to still the storms of nature and of evil are revealed in Jesus.

* *Epistle:* Christ came as an instrument of God's reconciliation with humanity.

### Phrases for highlighting and memorization

* "Who shut in the sea with doors when it burst out from the womb?" (Job 38:8)
* "He stilled the storm to a whisper and quieted the waves of the sea." (Psalm 107:29)
* "So if anyone is in Christ, there is a new creation: everything old has passed away; see, everything has become new!" (2 Cor. 5:17)
* "And they were filled with great awe and said to one another, 'Who then is this, that even the wind and the sea obey him?'" (Mark 4:41)

### Key words, ideas, and concepts to explore

* God as creator;
* demons;
* exorcism;
* "if anyone is in Christ";
* "ministry of reconciliation";
* "ambassadors of Christ."

### Stories to tell

- ◆ The narrative portion of the book of Job that precedes and follows the great wisdom poetry of Job (Job 1:1–2:13; 42:7-17);
- ◆ The story of Jesus stilling the storm;
- ◆ The healing of the Gerasene demoniac.

### Christian practice and liturgical tradition

- ◆ Elements of exorcism continue in church practice today. See the provisions "Concerning Exorcism" in *The Book of Occasional Services.*
- ◆ Candidates renounce evil at their baptism (BCP 302).
- ◆ We ask God to "deliver us from evil" every time we offer the Lord's Prayer.
- ◆ Eucharistic Prayer B includes the phrase, "You have delivered us from evil and made us worthy to stand before you" (BCP 368).

### Formation in baptismal discipleship

The passing of the peace in the liturgy dramatizes the role of the Christian in the world. Reconciliation is expressed as an essential component in congregational life, which is precisely why the peace is shared every time Christians gather for eucharist. Evil is taken seriously in the liturgy, in counseling, and in social witness.


## Proper 8, Year B (The Sunday closest to June 29)

Lections: Deuteronomy 15:7-11; Psalm 112; 2 Corinthians 8:1-9, 13-15; Mark 5:22-24, 35b-43

### Theme of the lections

God's power to heal and bring life even out of death is revealed in Jesus.

- ◆ *Epistle:* A call for generosity.

### Phrases for highlighting and memorization

- ◆ "Since there will never cease to be some in need on the earth, I therefore command you, 'Open your hand to the poor and needy neighbor in your land.'" (Deut. 15:11)
- ◆ "Light shines in the darkness for the upright; the righteous are merciful and full of compassion." (Psalm 112:4)

- "For you know the generous act of our Lord Jesus Christ, that though he was rich, yet for your sakes he became poor, so that by his poverty you might become rich." (2 Cor. 8:9)
- "Jesus said to the leader of the synagogue, 'Do not fear, only believe.'" (Mark 5:36b)

### Key words, ideas, and concepts to explore
- healing;
- raising to life;
- stewardship;
- generosity;
- charity;
- alms.

### Stories to tell
- The healing of Jairus' daughter.

### Christian practice and liturgical tradition
- The offertory at the eucharist is a weekly call to generosity. Tithes and gifts are offered for the needs of others.
- The dismissal from the eucharist includes the exhortation to "Go in peace to love and serve the Lord."

### Formation in baptismal discipleship
Acts 2:43-47 describes a church in which everything was held in common and distributed to each person as needed. This vision of congregational life, as idealistic as it may seem, must shape the church's understanding of community, stewardship, and the Baptismal Covenant, which calls for the Christian to "seek and serve Christ in all persons" (BCP 305).

## Proper 9, Year B (The Sunday closest to July 6)
Lections: Ezekiel 2:1-7; Psalm 123; 2 Corinthians 12:2-10; Mark 6:1-6

### Theme of the lections
Jesus' rejection by his own people.
- *Epistle:* Paul finds Christ's power in the midst of weakness.

### Phrases for highlighting and memorization

- "You shall speak my words to them, whether they hear or refuse to hear; for they are a rebellious house." (Ezek. 2:7)
- "So our eyes look to the LORD our God, until he show us his mercy." (Psalm 123:3)
- "[The Lord] said to me, 'My grace is sufficient for you, for power is made perfect in weakness.'" (2 Cor. 12:9a)
- "Jesus said to them, 'Prophets are not without honor, except in their hometown, and among their own kin, and in their own house.'" (Mark 6:4)

### Key words, ideas, and concepts to explore

- prophet;
- rejection of God's word;
- grace;
- power known in weakness.

### Formation in baptismal discipleship

The church that follows Christ will experience rejection and alienation.

## Proper 10, Year B (The Sunday closest to July 13)

Lections: Amos 7:7-15; Psalm 85:7-13; Ephesians 1:1-14; Mark 6:7-13

### Theme of the lections

The call to prophetic witness.

### Phrases for highlighting and memorization

- "And the LORD took me from following the flock, and the LORD said to me, 'Go, prophesy to my people Israel.'" (Amos 7:15)
- "I will listen to what the LORD God is saying, for he is speaking peace to his faithful people and to those who turn their hearts to him." (Psalm 85:8)
- "In Christ we have also obtained an inheritance...so that we, who were the first to set our hope on Christ, might live for the praise of his glory." (Eph. 1:11-12)
- "He called the twelve and began to send them out two by two." (Mark 6:7a)

### Key words, ideas, and concepts to explore

- unclean spirits;
- anointing;
- healing;
- exorcism;
- repentance;
- plumb line;
- sealed by the Holy Spirit;
- This week begins an eight-week, semi-continuous reading of Ephesians. Take time to introduce the epistle as an educational offering.

### Christian practice and liturgical tradition

- The practice of anointing the sick is provided for in "Ministration to the Sick" (BCP 455-456).
- Ephesians 1:13 ("marked with the seal of the promised Holy Spirit") and other texts lie behind the anointing at baptism: "You are sealed by the Holy Spirit in Baptism and marked as Christ's own forever" (BCP 308).

## Proper 11, Year B (The Sunday closest to July 20)

Lections: Isaiah 57:14b-21; Psalm 22:22-30; Ephesians 2:11-22; Mark 6:30-44

### Theme of the lections

Jesus' compassion for the people leads him to respond with food for mind and body. The feeding of the five thousand expresses the significance of the Holy Eucharist. This eucharistic theme will be carried on in Propers 13, 14, 15, and 16, Year B.

- *Epistle:* The Christian is the living temple of God in the world.

### Phrases for highlighting and memorisation

- "For thus says the high and lofty one who inhabits eternity, whose name is Holy: I dwell in the high and holy place, and also with those who are contrite and humble in spirit, to revive the spirit of the humble, and to revive the heart of the contrite." (Isa. 57:15)
- "The poor shall eat and be satisfied, and those who seek the LORD shall praise him: 'May your heart live for ever!'" (Psalm 22:25)
- "But now in Christ Jesus you who once were far off have been brought near by the blood of Christ." (Eph. 2:13)

♦ "As he went ashore, he saw a great crowd; and he had compassion for them, because they were like sheep without a shepherd; and he began to teach them many things." (Mark 6:34)

### Key words, ideas, and concepts to explore
- ♦ bread (manna);
- ♦ eucharistic actions (took bread, blessed, broke, gave);
- ♦ blood of Christ;
- ♦ reconciliation;
- ♦ peace;
- ♦ household of God;
- ♦ foundation of the apostles;
- ♦ dwelling place of God in the Spirit;
- ♦ the temple as the meeting place between God and the people.

### Stories to tell
- ♦ The feeding of the five thousand.

### Christian practice and liturgical tradition
- ♦ There are eucharistic overtones to this day's gospel story. Jesus "took bread, blessed the bread, broke it, and distributed it among the people." Notice that Jesus "feeds" the people first with teaching and then with bread. At the eucharist we first hear the word and then receive the eucharistic bread: word and sacrament lie at the heart of the Christian life.

### Formation in baptismal discipleship
Christ has compassion for the people of the church and the world who hunger for God's word.

## Proper 12, Year B (The Sunday closest to July 27)
Lections: 2 Kings 2:1-15; Psalm 114; Ephesians 4:1-7, 11-16; Mark 6:45-52

### Theme of the lections
God's power is revealed in Elijah and Jesus as the waters are parted and calmed.
- ♦ *Epistle:* Christians are all part of the one Body and the one Spirit in Christ.

*Phrases for highlighting and memorization*

- "He took the mantle of Elijah that had fallen from him, and struck the water, saying, 'Where is the LORD, the God of Elijah?' When he had struck the water, the water was parted to the one side and to the other, and Elisha went over." (2 Kings 2:14)
- "The sea beheld it and fled; Jordan turned and went back." (Psalm 114:3)
- "There is one body and one Spirit, just as you were called to the one hope of your calling, one Lord, one faith, one baptism, one God and Father of all, who is above all and through all and in all." (Eph. 4:4-6)
- "But when they saw him walking on the sea, they thought it was a ghost and cried out; for they all saw him and were terrified. But immediately he spoke to them and said, 'Take heart, it is I; do not be afraid.'" (Mark 6:49-50)

*Key words, ideas, and concepts to explore*

- prophet;
- Elijah and Elisha;
- God's power over the waters (beginning with Genesis 1).

*Stories to tell*

- The story of Elijah's ascension and Elisha's succession as prophet;
- The story of Jesus walking on the water.

*Christian practice and liturgical tradition*

- The words of greeting in the baptismal rite (BCP 299) are taken from today's reading from Ephesians.

*Formation in baptismal discipleship*

The congregation values the gifts of ministry of all the baptized. All have gifts and are integral members of the Body of Christ.

# Proper 13, Year B (The Sunday closest to August 3)

Lections: Exodus 16:2-4, 9-15; Psalm 78:14-20, 23-25; Ephesians 4:17-25; John 6:24-35

### Theme of the lections

A continuation of the eucharistic theme from Proper 11, Year B. Jesus is the bread of heaven. (See Propers 11, 14, 15, and 16, Year B.)

- *Epistle:* Put on the new nature of Christ and let go of the old nature of alienation.

### Phrases for highlighting and memorization

- "When the Israelites saw it, they said to one another, 'What is it?' For they did not know what it was. Moses said to them, 'It is the bread that the LORD has given you to eat.'" (Exod. 16:15)
- "He rained down manna upon them to eat and gave them grain from heaven." (Psalm 78:24)
- "Clothe yourselves with the new self, created according to the likeness of God in true righteousness and holiness." (Eph. 4:24)
- "Jesus said to them, 'I am the bread of life. Whoever comes to me will never be hungry, and whoever believes in me will never be thirsty.'" (John 6:35)

### Key words, ideas, and concepts to explore

- eucharistic actions (took bread, blessed, broke, gave);
- manna;
- bread of life;
- put on the new nature of Christ.

### Stories to tell

- The feeding of the Israelites in the wilderness.

### Christian practice and liturgical tradition

- In the eucharist we are given the bread "which comes down from heaven and gives life to the world" (John 6:33).

### Formation in baptismal discipleship

In celebrating the Holy Eucharist week by week we both participate in and receive the Body of Christ.

# Proper 14, Year B (The Sunday closest to August 10)

Lections: Deuteronomy 8:1-10; Psalm 34:1-8; Ephesians 4:(25-29) 30–5:2; John 6:37-51

### Theme of the lections

A continuation of the Bread of Life theme. (See Propers 11, 13, 15, and 16, Year B.)

- *Epistle:* Instruction about communal life in the church.

### Phrases for highlighting and memorization

- "He humbled you by letting you hunger, then by feeding you with manna, with which neither you nor your ancestors were acquainted, in order to make you understand that one does not live by bread alone, but by every word that comes from the mouth of the LORD." (Deut. 8:3)
- "Taste and see that LORD is good; happy are they who trust in him!" (Psalm 34:8)
- "Live in love, as Christ loved us and gave himself up for us, a fragrant offering and sacrifice to God." (Eph. 5:2)
- "I am the living bread that came down from heaven. Whoever eats of this bread will live forever; and the bread that I will give for the life of the world is my flesh." (John 6:51)

### Key words, ideas, and concepts to explore

- manna;
- Jesus, the Bread of Life;
- "sealed by the Holy Spirit."

### Christian practice and liturgical tradition

- The ancient rite of anointing in baptism reflects the epistle for today: *"N., you are sealed by the Holy Spirit in Baptism and marked as Christ's own for ever."* (BCP 308)

### Formation in baptismal discipleship

The letter to the Ephesians reminds us that Christians are called to "live in love, as Christ loved us," to be kind and tenderhearted in our forgiveness of one another.

## Proper 15, Year B (The Sunday closest to August 17)

Lections: Proverbs 9:1-6; Psalm 147 or Psalm 34:9-14; Ephesians 5:15-20; John 6:53-59

### Theme of the lections

A continuation of the Bread of Life theme. (See Propers 11, 13, 14, and 16, Year B). God's Word (*Logos*, Wisdom) brings the life-giving knowledge of God. God's Word is the very bread of life.

 ◆ *Epistle:* Live as a new people, giving up your old ways.

### Phrases for highlighting and memorization

 ◆ "Come, eat of my bread and drink of the wine I have mixed." (Prov. 9:5)
 ◆ "He declares his word to Jacob, his statutes and his judgments to Israel." (Psalm 147:20)
 ◆ "Be filled with the Spirit, as you sing psalms and hymns and spiritual songs among yourselves, singing and making melody to the Lord in your hearts. (Eph. 5:18b-19)
 ◆ "Those who eat my flesh and drink my blood abide in me, and I in them." (John 6:56)

### Key words, ideas, and concepts to explore

 ◆ God's wisdom personified as a woman calling to the townspeople;
 ◆ *Logos;*
 ◆ psalms, hymns, spiritual songs;
 ◆ the flesh and blood of Christ.

### Christian practice and liturgical tradition

 ◆ The wonderful heritage of hymnody is expressed in the reading from Ephesians.
 ◆ The writer of the gospel of John sees Jesus as the incarnation of God's Wisdom, who came to humanity in the flesh of Jesus to reveal God's Word by living it fully among people:

> *In the beginning was the Word, and the Word was with God, and the Word was God....And the Word became flesh and lived among us.* (John 1:1, 14a)

# Proper 16, Year B (The Sunday closest to August 24)

Lections: Joshua 24:1-2a, 14-25; Psalm 16 or 34:15-22; Ephesians 5:21-33; John 6:60-69

### Theme of the lections

The conclusion of the Bread of Life theme from Propers 11, 13, 14, and 15, Year B, with the disciples' response to Jesus' pronouncement that he is the "bread of life."

- *Epistle:* Guidelines for marriage in the church.

### Phrases for highlighting and memorization

- "And with him ten chiefs, one from each of the tribal families of Israel, every one of them the head of a family among the clans of Israel." (Josh. 22:14)
- "Protect me, O God, for I take refuge in you; I have said to the LORD, 'You are my Lord, my good above all other.'" (Psalm 16:1)
- "Be subject to one another out of reverence for Christ." (Eph. 5:21)
- "The words that I have spoken to you are spirit and life." (John 6:63b)

### Key words, ideas, and concepts to explore

- discipleship;
- bread of life;
- calling into covenant relationship.

### Stories to tell

- The covenant ceremony at Shechem (Joshua 24).

### Christian practice and liturgical tradition

- The baptismal rite expresses the sense of call heard in the reading from Joshua ("I present N. to receive the Sacrament of Baptism") and the theme of choice ("Do you desire to be baptized?"). To be baptized is to enter into an eternal covenant with God.

### Formation in baptismal discipleship

Christians are called in baptism into an eternal covenant with God.

## Proper 17, Year B (The Sunday closest to August 31)

Lections: Deuteronomy 4:1-9; Psalm 15; Ephesians 6:10-20; Mark 7:1-8, 14-15, 21-23

### Theme of the lections

Honoring the commandments of the Torah above pious empty practices.

- *Epistle:* The need to be strong in the face of evil.

### Phrases for highlighting and memorization

- "You must neither add anything to what I command you nor take away anything from it, but keep the commandments of the LORD your God with which I am charging you." (Deut. 4:2)
- "LORD, who may dwell in your tabernacle? Who may abide upon your holy hill?" (Psalm 15:1)
- "Therefore take up the whole armor of God, so that you may be able to withstand on that evil day, and having done everything, to stand firm." (Eph. 6:13)
- "There is nothing outside a person that by going in can defile, but the things that come out are what defile." (Mark 7:15)

### Key words, ideas, and concepts to explore

- "armor of God";
- commandments;
- ceremonial traditions of the Pharisees.

### Formation in baptismal discipleship

In a church that finds meaning in ceremonial ritual worship, it is important always to examine those practices in the light of this Sunday's lessons.


## Proper 18, Year B (The Sunday closest to September 7)

Lections: Isaiah 35:4-7a; Psalm 146:4-9; James 1:17-27; Mark 7:31-37

### Theme of the lections

Jesus as a sign of the dawning of God's reign.

- *Epistle:* Be doers and not merely hearers of God's word.

### Phrases for highlighting and memorization

- "'[God] will come and save you.' Then the eyes of the blind shall be opened and the ears of the deaf unstopped." (Isa. 35:4c-5)
- "The LORD sets the prisoners free; the LORD opens the eyes of the blind; the LORD lifts up those who are bowed down." (Psalm 146:7)
- "Be doers of the word, and not merely hearers who deceive themselves." (James 1:22)
- "They were astounded beyond measure, saying, 'He has done everything well; he even makes the deaf to hear and the mute to speak.'" (Mark 7:37)

### Key words, ideas, and concepts to explore

- "doers of the word";
- first fruits;
- the kingdom of God;
- This week begins a four-week, semi-continuous reading of James. Take time to set the stage for the hearing of this epistle.

### Stories to tell

- The healing of the deaf man with a speech impediment.

### Christian practice and liturgical tradition

- We pray for God's kingdom to come every time we pray the Lord's Prayer.

## Proper 19, Year B (The Sunday closest to September 14)

Lections: Isaiah 50:4-9; Psalm 116:1-8; James 2:1-5, 8-10, 14-18; Mark 8:27-38 or Mark 9:14-29

### Theme of the lections

Peter recognizes Jesus as the Christ. The cost of discipleship includes bearing the cross. (Alternative gospel text, Mark 9:14-29: Jesus heals a child with an "unclean spirit.")

- *Epistle:* Faith is shown by one's actions, especially in showing compassion.

### Phrases for highlighting and memorization

- "The Lord GOD has given me the tongue of a teacher, that I may know how to sustain the weary with a word. Morning by morning he wakens—wakens my ear to listen as those who are taught." (Isa. 50:4)
- "I will walk in the presence of the LORD in the land of the living." (Psalm 116:8)
- "What good is it, my brothers and sisters, if you say you have faith but do not have works? Can faith save you?" (James 2:14)
- "He called the crowd with his disciples, and said to them, 'If any want to become my followers, let them deny themselves and take up their cross and follow me.'" (Mark 8:34)

### Key words, ideas, and concepts to explore

- "doers of the word";
- faith and works;
- Christ/Messiah;
- Satan;
- taking up the cross.

### Stories to tell

- The healing of the possessed boy (in the alternative gospel lesson).

### Formation in baptismal discipleship

Christian congregations must practice hospitality to all people, with an imperative to reach out to the poor. The call to respond to human need comes directly from scripture and the Baptismal Covenant.

## Proper 20, Year B (The Sunday closest to September 21)

Lections: Wisdom of Solomon 1:16–2:1(6-11)12-22; Psalm 54; James 3:16–4:6; Mark 9:30-37

### Theme of the lections

Jesus predicts his passion a second time and reminds his disciples that to be great in the kingdom of God is to be the servant of all.

- *Epistle:* The church must live by the values of the gospel, not of the world.

### Phrases for highlighting and memorization

- "The very sight of him is a burden to us, because his manner of life is unlike that of others, and his ways are strange." (Wisd. of Sol. 2:15)
- "For the arrogant have risen up against me, and the ruthless have sought my life, those who have no regard for God." (Psalm 54:3)
- "For where there is envy and selfish ambition, there will also be disorder and wickedness of every kind." (James 3:16)
- "Whoever wants to be first must be last of all and servant of all." (Mark 9:35b)

### Key words, ideas, and concepts to explore

- servant of all;
- Son of Man;
- wisdom;
- envy and selfish ambition;
- friendship with the world.

### Stories to tell

- The story of Jesus welcoming a child.

### Christian practice and liturgical tradition

- The tradition of footwashing on Maundy Thursday dramatizes Jesus' words in today's gospel text about servanthood.
- Jesus' passion, suffering, and death are remembered every time the Holy Eucharist is celebrated. The eucharist proclaims Jesus' servant ministry as a way of life.

### Formation in baptismal discipleship

The first in God's kingdom will be least of all and servant of all. Jesus' life of witness to God's way raises hostility among those who feel judged by his life. God's wisdom often runs counter to the world's wisdom.

## Proper 21, Year B (The Sunday closest to September 28)

Lections: Numbers 11:4-6, 10-16, 24-29; Psalm 19:7-14; James 4:7-12 (13–5:6); Mark 9:38-43, 45, 47-48

### Theme of the lections

Jesus' power breaks out in spontaneous acts of healing that cannot be confined to the church.

- *Epistle:* Live humbly and do not dare to judge one another.

### Phrases for highlighting and memorization

- "Then the LORD came down in the cloud and spoke to him, and took some of the spirit that was on him and put it on the seventy elders." (Num. 11:25a)
- "Above all, keep your servant from presumptuous sins; let them not get dominion over me; then shall I be whole and sound, and innocent of a great offense." (Psalm 19:13)
- "Do not speak evil against one another, brothers and sisters." (James 4:11a)
- "But Jesus said, 'Do not stop him; for no one who does a deed of power in my name will be able soon afterward to speak evil of me.'" (Mark 9:39)

### Key words, ideas, and concepts to explore

- the power of Jesus' name;
- living righteously;
- judgment;
- submission to God;
- receiving power and authority for ministry.

### Stories to tell

- The story of the manna from the book of Numbers.

### Christian practice and liturgical tradition

- The passing of the peace calls the church to live out God's forgiveness in the life of the community.
- At the eucharist all confess their sin and separation before God and all receive forgiveness; it is God who judges and forgives.

## Proper 22, Year B (The Sunday closest to October 5)

Lections: Genesis 2:18-24; Psalm 8 or 128; Hebrews 2:(1-8) 9-18; Mark 10:2-9

### Theme of the lections

The sanctity of the marriage relationship.

- *Epistle:* Because Christ shared so completely in everything that we suffer, Christ is the perfect high priest who "made us worthy to stand" before God (Eucharistic Prayer B, BCP 368).

### Phrases for highlighting and memorization

- "Therefore a man leaves his father and his mother and clings to his wife, and they become one flesh." (Gen. 2:24)
- "What is man that you should be mindful of him? the son of man that you should seek him out?" (Psalm 8:5)
- "Therefore he had to become like his brothers and sisters in every respect, so that he might be a merciful and faithful high priest in the service of God, to make a sacrifice of atonement for the sins of the people." (Heb. 2:17)
- "'For this reason a man shall leave his father and mother and be joined to his wife, and the two shall become one flesh.' So they are no longer two, but one flesh." (Mark 10:7-8)

### Key words, ideas, and concepts to explore

- Christ as high priest;
- temple sacrifices;
- marriage;
- the sacredness of human relationships;
- A seven-week, semi-continuous reading of the first ten chapters of Hebrews begins this Sunday. Take time to introduce this epistle, and to provide an understanding of the temple priesthood and sacrificial system.

### Christian practice and liturgical tradition

- The Celebration and Blessing of a Marriage (BCP 423-434) reflects the principles set forth in today's lections. Though marriage is a sacred relationship, the church recognizes the necessity of divorce where a couple cannot live into the commitment they made. It is expected that counseling, continuing concern, and repentance will be a part of Christian divorce.

- The eucharistic prayers of *The Book of Common Prayer* reflect the sacrificial language of Hebrews:

  *You...sent Jesus Christ...to share our human nature, to live and die as one of us, to reconcile us to you, the God and Father of all. He stretched out his arms upon the cross, and offered himself, in obedience to your will, a perfect sacrifice for the whole world.* (BCP 362)

### Formation in baptismal discipleship

The sacredness of marriage in today's lections and in the marriage rite of *The Book of Common Prayer* expresses the sacredness of *all* relationships before God: "God is love, and those who abide in love abide in God, and God abides in them" (1 John 4:16b).

## Proper 23, Year B (The Sunday closest to October 12)

Lections: Amos 5:6-7, 10-15; Psalm 90:1-8, 12; Hebrews 3:1-6; Mark 10:17-27 (28-31)

### Theme of the lections

The desire for wealth can lead to injustice, lack of compassion, and estrangement from God.

- *Epistle:* As Jesus was like a son in the household of God, so we are daughters and sons in God's household.

### Phrases for highlighting and memorization

- "Therefore because you trample on the poor and take from them levies of grain, you have built houses of hewn stone, but you shall not live in them; you have planted pleasant vineyards, but you shall not drink their wine." (Amos 5:11)
- "So teach us to number our days that we may apply our hearts to wisdom." (Psalm 90:12)
- "Christ, however, was faithful over God's house as a son, and we are his house if we hold firm the confidence and the pride that belong to hope." (Heb. 3:6)
- "Go, sell what you own, and give the money to the poor, and you will have treasure in heaven; then come, follow me." (Mark 10:21b)

### Key words, ideas, and concepts to explore

- justice and the acquisition of wealth;

- stewardship;
- total commitment to God.

### Christian practice and liturgical tradition
- The monastic tradition models a total dedication to God by requiring its members to live simply and hold all goods in common.

### Formation in baptismal discipleship
Stewardship is a life lived for God rather than for social and economic advantage.


## Proper 24, Year B (The Sunday closest to October 19)
Lections: Isaiah 53:4-12; Psalm 91:9-16; Hebrews 4:12-16; Mark 10:35-45

### Theme of the lections
God calls the Christian into servant ministry, which means sharing in the suffering of others in order to bring life and healing.
- *Epistle:* Jesus as our great high priest.

### Phrases for highlighting and memorization
- "Surely he has borne our infirmities and carried our diseases; yet we accounted him stricken, struck down by God, and afflicted." (Isa. 53:4)
- "He shall call upon me, and I will answer him; I am with him in trouble; I will rescue him and bring him to honor." (Psalm 91:15)
- "Let us therefore approach the throne of grace with boldness, so that we may receive mercy and find grace to help in time of need." (Heb. 4:16)
- "Whoever wishes to be first among you must be slave of all. For the Son of Man came not to be served but to serve, and to give his life a ransom for many." (Mark 10:44-45)

### Key words, ideas, and concepts to explore
- suffering servant (the four servant songs of Isaiah);
- servant ministry;
- "life a ransom for many";
- Jesus as high priest.

*Christian practice and liturgical tradition*
- The role of deacon expresses the servant ministry of all the baptized. At ordination, the candidate hears these words from the bishop: *In the name of Jesus Christ, you are to serve all people, particularly the poor, the weak, the sick and the lonely....You are to interpret to the Church the needs, concerns, and hopes of the world.* (BCP 543)

*Formation in baptismal discipleship*
The congregation must take seriously its role to be servant to the world. Members need to be trained and encouraged to engage in servant ministry through their work and in their community.

## Proper 25, Year B (The Sunday closest to October 26)
Lections: Isaiah 59:(1-4) 9-19; Psalm 13; Hebrews 5:12–6:1, 9-12; Mark 10:46-52

*Theme of the lections*
Jesus comes to proclaim God's new day where people who are physically and metaphorically blind to injustice will see clearly the way of God.
- *Epistle:* A challenge to live faithfully and to seek a mature relationship with Christ.

*Phrases for highlighting and memorization*
- "Therefore justice is far from us, and righteousness does not reach us; we wait for light, and lo! there is darkness; and for brightness, but we walk in gloom." (Isa. 59:9)
- "Look upon me and answer me, O LORD my God; give light to my eyes, lest I sleep in death." (Psalm 13:3)
- "Therefore let us go on toward perfection, leaving behind the basic teaching about Christ." (Heb. 6:1a)
- "Jesus said to him, 'Go; your faith has made you well.' Immediately he regained his sight and followed him on the way." (Mark 10:52)

*Key words, ideas, and concepts to explore*
- healing;
- seeking maturity in faith;
- blindness as a metaphor for turning from God's covenant.

*Formation in baptismal discipleship*

A congregation needs to ask constantly where it is blind to human need and to God's call to live by the Baptismal Covenant.

## Proper 26, Year B (The Sunday closest to November 2)

Lections: Deuteronomy 6:1-9; Psalm 119:1-8; Hebrews 7:23-28; Mark 12:28-34

### Theme of the lections

Loving God and neighbor are the greatest commandments.

- *Epistle:* Jesus is our perfect high priest.

### Phrases for highlighting and memorization

- "Hear, O Israel: The LORD is our God, the LORD alone. You shall love the LORD your God with all your heart, and with all your soul, and with all your might." (Deut. 6:4-5)
- "Happy are they whose way is blameless, who walk in the law of the LORD!" (Psalm 119:1)
- "Consequently [Christ] is able for all time to save those who approach God through him, since he always lives to make intercession for them." (Heb. 7:25)
- "Jesus answered, 'The first is, "Hear, O Israel: the Lord our God, the Lord is one; you shall love the Lord your God with all your heart, and with all your soul, and with all your mind, and with all your strength."'" (Mark 12:29-30)

### Key words, ideas, and concepts to explore

- high priest;
- loving God and neighbor;
- the *Shema* (from Deuteronomy).

### Christian practice and liturgical tradition

- The commandment to love God and neighbor is part of the optional penitential order before the eucharist (BCP 319, 351; see also 324).
- The "loving neighbor as self" commandment is also reflected in the Baptismal Covenant: "Will you seek and serve Christ in all persons, loving your neighbor as yourself?" (BCP 305).

*Formation in baptismal discipleship*

The commandments to love God and neighbor serve as a way of measuring a congregation's faithfulness to the gospel.

## Proper 27, Year B (The Sunday closest to November 9)

Lections: 1 Kings 17:8-16; Psalm 146:4-9; Hebrews 9:24-28; Mark 12:38-44

*Theme of the lections*

The offering of two impoverished women is a witness to true faith in God. (Note: The themes of the season of Advent begin to be expressed this week, offering an opportunity to explore the rich heritage of Advent. This week all three readings focus on the coming of Christ in glory and on the last judgment.)

◆ *Epistle:* Christ as will appear as high priest before the world a second time to fulfill the sacred role.

*Phrases for highlighting and memorization*

◆ "She went and did as Elijah said, so that she as well as he and her household ate for many days." (1 Kings 17:15)

◆ "The LORD loves the righteous; the LORD cares for the stranger; he sustains the orphan and widow, but frustrates the way of the wicked." (Psalm 146:8)

◆ "So Christ, having been offered once to bear the sins of many, will appear a second time, not to deal with sin, but to save those who are eagerly waiting for him." (Heb. 9:28)

◆ "For all of them have contributed out of their abundance; but she out of her poverty has put in everything she had, all she had to live on." (Mark 12:44)

*Key words, ideas, and concepts to explore*

◆ high priest;
◆ offering;
◆ offertory at the eucharist;
◆ stewardship.

*Stories to tell*

◆ The widow of Zarephath;
◆ The poor widow in the gospel text.

### Christian practice and liturgical tradition

♦ The offertory at the eucharist expresses the theme of self-offering in today's lections. The call for total self-offering is reflected in the eucharistic prayers of the Prayer Book:

*And here we offer and present unto thee, O Lord, our selves, our souls and bodies, to be a reasonable, holy, and living sacrifice unto thee.*" (BCP 336)

### Formation in baptismal discipleship

Stewardship is a way of life, not a fundraising campaign.


## Proper 28, Year B (The Sunday closest to November 16)

Lections: Daniel 12:1-4a (5-13); Psalm 16:5-11; Hebrews 10:31-39; Mark 13:14-23

### Theme of the lections

The coming day of glory and judgment is ushered in by a time of frightening upheaval and persecution.

### Phrases for highlighting and memorization

♦ "There shall be a time of anguish, such as has never occurred since nations first came into existence. But at that time your people shall be delivered, everyone who is found written in the book." (Dan. 12:1b)

♦ "For you will not abandon me to the grave, nor let your holy one see the Pit." (Psalm 16:10)

♦ "But we are not among those who shrink back and so are lost, but among those who have faith and so are saved." (Heb. 10:39)

♦ "For in those days there will be suffering, such as has not been from the beginning of the creation that God created until now, no, and never will be." (Mark 13:19)

### Key words, ideas, and concepts to explore

♦ Apocalyptic literature is heard during this pre-Advent and the Advent season. This style of literature uses poetry and rich imagery to emphasize that suffering and struggle lead to God's final intervention at the end of the present age. God will come to usher in the kingdom of God, a time when God's full sovereignty is known "on earth as in heaven." Apocalyptic literature gives hope to a church under persecution, for the struggles of the present moment are a sign that God's reign is indeed coming. Persecution and suffering are not the end, but the beginning. God's kingdom brings the promise of judgment and salvation. It may arrive at any time, so the church must always be ready. See An Outline of the Faith, section "The Christian Hope" (BCP 861-862).

### Christian practice and liturgical tradition
- The creeds and prayers of *The Book of Common Prayer* express the theme of God's coming promise and judgment:

  *He will come again to judge the living and the dead.* (Apostles' Creed, BCP 96)

  *He will come again in glory to judge the living and the dead, and his kingdom will have no end.* (Nicene Creed, BCP 359)

  *Therefore we proclaim the mystery of faith. Christ has died. Christ is risen. Christ will come again.* (BCP 363)

### Formation in baptismal discipleship
The congregation lives in the light of the resurrection and the final judgment. Hope and judgment characterize the outlook of the church as it proclaims Christ to the world.


## Proper 29, Year B (The Sunday closest to November 23)
Lections: Daniel 7:9-14; Psalm 93; Revelation 1:1-8; John 18:33-37 or Mark 11:1-11

### Theme of the lections
This day is often referred to as the Sunday of Christ the King, or Reign of Christ. Christ's sovereignty is the major theme in the lections for all three years.

(Note: Mark 11:1-11, Jesus' triumphal entry into Jerusalem, is an alternative gospel lection. This option also reflects the theme of Christ the King with its clear allusion to Zechariah 9:9: "Lo, your king comes to you; triumphant and victorious is he, humble and riding on a donkey, on a colt, the foal of a donkey.")

### Phrases for highlighting and memorization
- "As I watched in the night visions, I saw one like a human being coming with the clouds of heaven. And he came to the Ancient One and was presented before him. To him was given dominion and glory and

kingship, that all peoples, nations, and languages should serve him. His dominion is an everlasting dominion that shall not pass away, and his kingship is one that shall never be destroyed." (Dan. 7:13-14)

◆ "The LORD is King; he has put on splendid apparel; the LORD has put on his apparel and girded himself with strength." (Psalm 93:1)

◆ "John to the seven churches that are in Asia: Grace to you and peace from him who is and who was and who is to come, and from the seven spirits who are before his throne, and from Jesus Christ, the faithful witness, the firstborn of the dead, and the ruler of the kings of the earth. To him who loves us and freed us from our sins by his blood...be glory and dominion forever and ever. Amen." (Rev. 1:4-5, 6b)

◆ "Pilate asked him, 'So you are a king?' Jesus answered, 'You say that I am a king. For this I was born, and for this I came into the world, to testify to the truth. Everyone who belongs to the truth listens to my voice.'" (John 18:37)

### Key words, ideas, and concepts to explore

◆ Christ as king or sovereign;
◆ Daniel;
◆ everlasting dominion;
◆ testifying to the truth.

### Christian practice and liturgical tradition

◆ Some of the traditions associated with worship in the Episcopal Church have their origins in the royal court: for example, purple, the color for Advent and Lent, was the color associated with royalty and became linked to the coming of Christ as king.
◆ The psalms and prayers of the church are filled with imagery of the ruler.

### Formation in baptismal discipleship

"Jesus is Lord" (the earliest Christian creed) means that Jesus stands above all other earthly power and authority. All through history and into the present moment, choosing God above earthly authority has caused persecution and conflict in the life of the church. The congregation and wider church must witness always to the authority of Jesus Christ, realizing that there will be times when conflict will be the direct result of such a witness.

## Proper 4, Year C (The Sunday closest to June 1)

Lections: 1 Kings 8:22-23, 27-30, 41-43; Psalm 96:1-9; Galatians 1:1-10; Luke 7:1-10

### Theme of the lections

God's power and presence are revealed to the foreigner.

- *Epistle:* Paul writes to the church at Galatia, "Stick with the message I taught you. Don't accept a substitute!"

### Phrases for highlighting and memorization

- "When a foreigner comes and prays toward this house, then hear in heaven your dwelling place, and do according to all that the foreigner calls to you, so that all the peoples of the earth may know your name and fear you, as do your people Israel." (1 Kings 8:42b-43a)
- "Declare his glory among the nations and his wonders among all peoples." (Psalm 96:3)
- "If anyone proclaims to you a gospel contrary to what you received, let that one be accursed!" (Gal. 1:9b)
- "When Jesus heard this he was amazed at him, and turning to the crowd that followed him, he said, 'I tell you, not even in Israel have I found such faith.'" (Luke 7:9)

### Key words, ideas, and concepts to explore

- temple;
- intercessory prayer;
- God's "dwelling place";
- faith;
- healing;
- grace;
- gospel;
- This week begins a six-week, semi-continuous reading of Galatians. Provide an overview of the epistle to provide a context.

### Stories to tell

- Solomon's temple dedication;
- The healing of the centurion's servant.

### Christian practice and liturgical tradition
◆ Intercessions are a part of every worship service.

### Formation in baptismal discipleship
The church is a people called into prayer. Personal prayer flows out of public (liturgical) prayer. The church gathers in prayer and then goes out into the world to enact the prayers in actions of service and justice.

## Proper 5, Year C (The Sunday closest to June 8)
Lections: 1 Kings 17:17-24; Psalm 30:1-6, 12-13; Galatians 1:11-24; Luke 7:11-17

### Theme of the lections
God comes to bring life even out of death.
◆ *Epistle:* Paul defends his authority as an apostle.

### Phrases for highlighting and memorization
◆ "Elijah took the child, brought him down from the upper chamber into the house, and gave him to his mother; then Elijah said, 'See, your son is alive.'" (1 Kings 17:23)
◆ "You brought me up, O LORD, from the dead; you restored my life as I was going down to the grave." (Psalm 30:3)
◆ "They only heard it said, 'The one who formerly was persecuting us is now proclaiming the faith he once tried to destroy.'" (Gal. 1:23)
◆ "Fear seized all of them; and they glorified God, saying, 'A great prophet has risen among us!' and 'God has looked favorably on his people!'" (Luke 7:16)

### Key words, ideas, and concepts to explore
◆ healing;
◆ raising to life;
◆ word of the Lord;
◆ funeral practices of biblical times;
◆ prophecy;
◆ grace;
◆ preaching;
◆ Jerusalem as first center of apostolic authority;
◆ trace Paul's activities on a map or through photos or images of the geographical area.

### Stories to tell
* The story of Elijah and the widow of Zarephath.

### Christian practice and liturgical tradition
* The Burial of the Dead and the church's prayers for those who have died recognize a "raising up" into the resurrection life. We pray as those with hope (see rubric, BCP 507).

### Formation in baptismal discipleship
Christians are formed through prayer and devotion to an awareness of the communion of saints, the "whole family of God, the living and the dead" (BCP 862).


## Proper 6, Year C (The Sunday closest to June 15)
Lections: 2 Samuel 11:26–12:10, 13-15; Psalm 32:1-8; Galatians 2:11-21; Luke 7:36-50

### Theme of the lections
The forgiveness of sins.
* *Epistle:* The Christian is justified through faith in Christ rather than by works of the Law.

### Phrases for highlighting and memorization
* "Nathan said to David, 'Now the LORD has put away your sin; you shall not die.'" (2 Sam. 12:13b)
* "Happy are they whose transgressions are forgiven, and whose sin is put away!" (Psalm 32:1)
* "I have been crucified with Christ; and it is no longer I who live, but it is Christ who lives in me. (Gal. 2:19b-20a)
* "Therefore, I tell you, her sins, which were many, have been forgiven; hence she has shown great love. But the one to whom little is forgiven, loves little." (Luke 7:47)

### Key words, ideas, and concepts to explore
* sin;
* forgiveness;
* repentance;
* justification;
* "crucified with Christ";

- "Christ lives in me";
- customs associated with hospitality in biblical times.

### Stories to tell
- A woman anoints the feet of Jesus.

### Christian practice and liturgical tradition
- The traditions associated with the footwashing on Maundy Thursday provide an experience of servant ministry.
- The understanding that "Christ dwells in us" expressed in the Prayer Book comes, in part, from the Galatians text: That we may be made "one body with him, that he may dwell in us, and we in him" (BCP 336).

### Formation in baptismal discipleship
Congregations practice hospitality as a way of welcoming stranger and visitor into the forgiving fellowship of the church.


## Proper 7, Year C (The Sunday closest to June 22)
Lections: Zechariah 12:8-10, 13:1; Psalm 63:1-8; Galatians 3:23-29; Luke 9:18-24

### Theme of the lections
The centrality of the cross in the life of the Christian.
- *Epistle:* All are one people in Jesus Christ.

### Phrases for highlighting and memorization
- "And I will pour out a spirit of compassion and supplication on the house of David and the inhabitants of Jerusalem, so that, when they look on the one whom they have pierced, they shall mourn for him, as one mourns for an only child, and weep bitterly over him, as one weeps over a firstborn." (Zech. 12:10)
- "My soul clings to you; your right hand holds me fast." (Psalm 63:8)
- "Now before faith came, we were imprisoned and guarded under the law until faith would be revealed." (Gal. 3:23)
- "Then he said to them all, 'If any want to become my followers, let them deny themselves and take up their cross daily and follow me.'" (Luke 9:23)

### Key words, ideas, and concepts to explore
- taking up the cross daily;
- "Christ of God";
- Son of Man;
- denying oneself;
- "putting on Christ";
- living by faith rather than by law.

### Christian practice and liturgical tradition
- The Good Friday tradition of meditating on the cross (BCP 281-282) is kept in many congregations.
- The cross is central to all aspects of the Christian tradition.

### Formation in baptismal discipleship
The church must bear the pain of injustice, oppression, and alienation as a sign of God's healing that is expressed in the cross.


## Proper 8, Year C (The Sunday closest to June 29)
Lections: 1 Kings 19:15-16, 19-21; Psalm 16:5-11; Galatians 5:1, 13-25; Luke 9:51-62

### Theme of the lections
Leaving everything to follow Christ.
- *Epistle:* Accepting the freedom of the gospel.

### Phrases for highlighting and memorization
- "Then [Elisha] set out and followed Elijah, and became his servant." (1 Kings 19:21c)
- "I have set the LORD always before me; because he is at my right hand I shall not fall." (Psalm 16:8)
- "If we live by the Spirit, let us also be guided by the Spirit." (Gal. 5:25)
- "When the days drew near for him to be taken up, he set his face to go to Jerusalem." (Luke 9:51)

### Key words, ideas, and concepts to explore
- discipleship;
- rejection of God's word;
- freedom of the gospel;
- living by the Spirit;

- fruits of the Spirit;
- We will be walking with Jesus on the way to Jerusalem and the cross from this week through Proper 26.

### Christian practice and liturgical tradition

- At the ministration of communion the congregation moves to the Holy Table to receive the sacrament. In a sense, this movement expresses the call of the gospel to follow Christ. In some traditions, worship includes an "altar call" when people are invited to come forward to dedicate their lives to Christ. Episcopalians have a weekly "altar call" at the ministration of the eucharist.

### Formation in baptismal discipleship

The congregation is called to look ahead to the coming reign of God rather than back with nostalgia to the past.


## Proper 9, Year C (The Sunday closest to July 6)

Lections: Isaiah 66:10-16; Psalm 66:1-8; Galatians 6:(1-10) 14-18; Luke 10:1-12, 16-20

### Theme of the lections

The mission of the disciples and the church.

- *Epistle:* Paul finds his whole life expressed in the cross.

### Phrases for highlighting and memorization

- "As a mother comforts her child, so I will comfort you; you shall be comforted in Jerusalem." (Isa. 66:13)
- "Come now and see the works of God, how wonderful he is in his doing toward all people." (Psalm 66:4)
- "May I never boast of anything except the cross of our Lord Jesus Christ, by which the world has been crucified to me, and I to the world." (Gal. 6:14)
- "Whoever listens to you listens to me, and whoever rejects you rejects me, and whoever rejects me rejects the one who sent me." (Luke 10:16)

### Key words, ideas, and concepts to explore

- God's peace;
- kingdom (or reign) of God;

- discipline of the disciple;
- judgment;
- circumcision;
- the cross;
- the "marks of Jesus" (suffering for the sake of the gospel);
- God's "motherly" comfort.

### Formation in baptismal discipleship
Paul becomes a model for the church, bearing the marks of the cross by accepting suffering in proclaiming the gospel.

## Proper 10, Year C (The Sunday closest to July 13)
Lections: Deuteronomy 30:9-14; Psalm 25:3-9; Colossians 1:1-14; Luke 10:25-37

### Theme of the lections
Doing God's word.
- *Epistle:* Thanksgiving for the Christian church at Colossae.

### Phrases for highlighting and memorization
- "No, the word is very near to you; it is in your mouth and in your heart for you to observe." (Deut. 30:14)
- "Show me your ways, O LORD, and teach me your paths." (Psalm 25:3)
- "For this reason, since the day we heard it, we have not ceased praying for you and asking that you may be filled with the knowledge of God's will in all spiritual wisdom and understanding." (Col. 1:9)
- "He answered, 'You shall love the Lord your God with all your heart, and with all your soul, and with all your strength, and with all your mind; and your neighbor as yourself.'" (Luke 10:27)

### Key words, ideas, and concepts to explore
- commandments;
- God's word;
- priests and Levites;
- neighbor;
- prayer;
- spiritual wisdom;
- bearing fruit;

• This week begins a four-week, semi-continuous reading of Colossians. Take time to introduce the epistle as an educational offering.

### Stories to tell
• The parable of the Good Samaritan.

### Christian practice and liturgical tradition
• Many hospitals and congregations are named "Good Samaritan," reflecting the compassion expressed in the gospel story.

### Formation in baptismal discipleship
Acts of mercy inform the life and prayers of the congregation. As the despised Samaritan responded to the man in need, the church recognizes God's presence in the lives of those often considered its enemies.

## Proper 11, Year C (The Sunday closest to July 20)
Lections: Genesis 18:1-10a (10b-14); Psalm 15; Colossians 1:21-29; Luke 10:38-42

### Theme of the lections
Hospitality leads to encounters with God.
• *Epistle:* The mystery of God's word has been revealed to the saints.

### Phrases for highlighting and memorization
• "Then one said, 'I will surely return to you in due season, and your wife Sarah shall have a son.' And Sarah was listening at the tent entrance behind him." (Gen. 18:10)
• "LORD, who may dwell in your tabernacle? Who may abide upon your holy hill?" (Psalm 15:1)
• "To them God chose to make known how great among the Gentiles are the riches of the glory of this mystery, which is Christ in you, the hope of glory." (Col. 1:27)
• "Now as they went on their way, he entered a certain village, where a woman named Martha welcomed him into her home." (Luke 10:38)

### Key words, ideas, and concepts to explore
• Holy Eucharist;
• hospitality;
• Abraham and Sarah;

- patriarchs and matriarchs in the book of Genesis;
- suffering in Christ's name;
- mystery;
- "Christ in you";
- hope of glory.

### Stories to tell
- The story of God's promise of a son to Abraham and Sarah.

### Christian practice and liturgical tradition
- The Great Fifty Days of Easter have traditionally been called *mystagogia,* a time when the mysteries of the faith are revealed to those who have been baptized at the Easter Vigil. Paul wrote about the "mystery" being revealed at last (Rom. 16:25), and in Eucharistic Prayer A we say, "Therefore we proclaim the mystery of faith..." (BCP 363).

### Formation in baptismal discipleship
The church expresses hospitality to friend and stranger, treating each visitor as a possible messenger of God.


## Proper 12, Year C (The Sunday closest to July 27)
Lections: Genesis 18:20-33; Psalm 138; Colossians 2:6-15; Luke 11:1-13

### Theme of the lections
The importance and power of prayer.
- *Epistle:* The Christian has been brought to the fullness of life in Christ.

### Phrases for highlighting and memorization
- "Then Abraham came near and said, 'Will you indeed sweep away the righteous with the wicked?'" (Gen. 18:23)
- "When I called, you answered me; you increased my strength within me." (Psalm 138:4)
- "For in him the whole fullness of deity dwells bodily." (Col. 2:9)
- "So I say to you, Ask, and it will be given you; search, and you will find; knock, and the door will be opened for you." (Luke 11:9)

*Key words, ideas, and concepts to explore*

- prayer;
- intercession;
- the Lord's Prayer (compare the two versions of the Lord's Prayer found in this Sunday's gospel and Matthew 6:9-13);
- receiving and living in Christ.

*Stories to tell*

- The story of Abraham's prayer in Genesis;
- The parable of the persistent friend.

*Christian practice and liturgical tradition*

- The origin of the Lord's Prayer is heard in today's gospel lection.

*Formation in baptismal discipleship*

Intercessory prayer must be at the heart of congregational life; a life of prayer leads to acts of prayer.


## Proper 13, Year C (The Sunday closest to August 3)

Lections: Ecclesiastes 1:12-14; 2:(1-7, 11) 18-23; Psalm 49:1-11; Colossians 3:(5-11) 12-17; Luke 12:13-21

*Theme of the lections*

One cannot place hope in wealth and status.

- *Epistle:* Guidelines for witnessing to the power of Christ's love in the daily life of the church.

*Phrases for highlighting and memorization*

- "I saw all the deeds that are done under the sun; and see, all is vanity and a chasing after wind." (Eccl. 1:14)
- "For we see that the wise die also; like the dull and stupid they perish and leave their wealth to those who come after them." (Psalm 49:9)
- "And whatever you do, in word or deed, do everything in the name of the Lord Jesus, giving thanks to God the Father through him." (Col. 3:17)
- "So it is with those who store up treasures for themselves but are not rich toward God." (Luke 12:21)

### Key words, ideas, and concepts to explore
- peace of Christ;
- God's chosen ones;
- God's wisdom;
- vanity;
- parable;
- "rich toward God";
- stewardship.

### Stories to tell
- The parable of the rich fool.

### Christian practice and liturgical tradition
- The ancient custom of clothing the newly baptized in white garments had the symbolic significance of "putting on the love of Christ" (Col. 3:9-14). Later this symbol of being clothed in Christ became associated with the vesting of the priest in preparation for the celebration of the eucharist.

### Formation in baptismal discipleship
Colossians provides a picture of the ideal communal life of the church, forming people into the Body of Christ.

## Proper 14, Year C (The Sunday closest to August 10)
Lections: Genesis 15:1-6; Psalm 33:12-15, 18-22; Hebrews 11:1-3 (4-7) 8-16; Luke 12:32-40

### Theme of the lections
Being righteous through faith.

### Phrases for highlighting and memorization
- "And he believed the LORD; and the LORD reckoned it to him as righteousness." (Gen. 15:6)
- "Behold, the eye of the LORD is upon those who fear him, on those who wait upon his love." (Psalm 33:18)
- "By faith Abraham obeyed when he was called to set out for a place that he was to receive as an inheritance; and he set out, not knowing where he was going." (Heb. 11:8)

- "Blessed are those slaves whom the master finds alert when he comes; truly I tell you, he will fasten his belt and have them sit down to eat, and he will come and serve them." (Luke 12:37)

### Key words, ideas, and concepts to explore
- righteousness through faith;
- Abraham;
- inheritance;
- This Sunday begins a four week, semi-continuous reading of Hebrews 11-13. Provide a background in the educational setting for this epistle. Hebrews can be difficult for the contemporary hearer to understand with its frequent allusions to temple practices and priesthood.

### Stories to tell
- The story of Abraham and Sarah.

### Christian practice and liturgical tradition
- Texts such as the gospel for today led, in part, to the monastic tradition of taking a vow of poverty as an expression of total commitment to Christ.


## Proper 15, Year C (The Sunday closest to August 17)
Lections: Jeremiah 23:23-29; Psalm 82; Hebrews 12:1-7 (8-10) 11-14; Luke 12:49-56

### Theme of the lections
The cost of discipleship means choosing God above all others even when it creates conflict and division.
- *Epistle:* We are surrounded by a cloud of witnesses who help us persevere in following Christ, the perfect example of faithful obedience to God.

### Phrases for highlighting and memorization
- "Who can hide in secret places so that I cannot see them? says the LORD. Do I not fill heaven and earth? says the LORD." (Jer. 23:24)
- "Arise, O God, and rule the earth, for you shall take all nations for your own." (Psalm 82:8)

- ◆ "Therefore, since we are surrounded by so great a cloud of witnesses, let us also lay aside every weight and the sin that clings so closely, and let us run with perseverance the race that is set before us." (Heb. 12:1)
- ◆ "You hypocrites! You know how to interpret the appearance of earth and sky, but why do you not know how to interpret the present time?" (Luke 12:56)

### Key words, ideas, and concepts to explore
- ◆ cloud of witnesses;
- ◆ communion of saints;
- ◆ discipline;
- ◆ judgment;
- ◆ casting fire upon earth;
- ◆ apocalyptic literature.

### Christian practice and liturgical tradition
- ◆ The role of confession and penitence in the life of the church is heightened by texts such as those we hear this day.

### Formation in baptismal discipleship:
The church lives expectantly ("Christ will come again"), constantly judging its life not by the norms of the present time, but by the ethic of the coming reign of God.


## Proper 16, Year C (The Sunday closest to August 24)
Lections: Isaiah 28:14-22; Psalm 46; Hebrews 12:18-19, 22-29; Luke 13:22-30

### Theme of the lections
Jesus demands a decision. To follow him means changing one's life and walking in his way. No one can take salvation for granted.

### Phrases for highlighting and memorization
- ◆ "And I will make justice the line, and righteousness the plummet; hail will sweep away the refuge of lies, and waters will overwhelm the shelter." (Isa. 28:17)
- ◆ "Be still, then, and know that I am God; I will be exalted among the nations; I will be exalted in the earth." (Psalm 46:11)

- "Therefore, since we are receiving a kingdom that cannot be shaken, let us give thanks, by which we offer to God an acceptable worship with reverence and awe; for indeed our God is a consuming fire." (Heb. 12:28-29)
- "Strive to enter through the narrow door; for many, I tell you, will try to enter and will not be able." (Luke 13:24)

### Key words, ideas, and concepts to explore
- judgment;
- surveying with a plumb line;
- Sheol;
- reverence;
- consuming fire;
- narrow door.

### Christian practice and liturgical tradition
- The Holy Eucharist is a "foretaste" of the messianic banquet.
- The confession of sin and acknowledgment of human sinfulness are integral parts of every eucharistic celebration.

### Formation in baptismal discipleship
The church must live within the tension of proclaiming the good news of God's forgiveness revealed through Christ, and the judgment associated with entering "through the narrow door."

## Proper 17, Year C (The Sunday closest to August 31)
Lections: Ecclesiasticus 10:(7-11)12-18; Psalm 112; Hebrews 13:1-8; Luke 14:1,7-14

### Theme of the lections
A call to compassion and a warning against pride.

### Phrases for highlighting and memorization
- "The Lord overthrows the thrones of rulers, and enthrones the lowly in their place." (Ecclesiasticus 10:14)
- "They have given freely to the poor, and their righteousness stands fast for ever; they will hold up their head with honor." (Psalm 112:9)
- "Now may the God of peace...make you complete in everything good so that you may do his will, working among us that which is pleasing

in his sight, through Jesus Christ, to whom be the glory forever and ever. Amen." (Heb. 13:20-21)
- ♦ "For all who exalt themselves will be humbled, and those who humble themselves will be exalted." (Luke 14:11)

### Key words, ideas, and concepts to explore
- ♦ biblical customs of hospitality;
- ♦ pride;
- ♦ exaltation and humility;
- ♦ compassion.

### Formation in baptismal discipleship
Hospitality must be the hallmark of the Christian congregation. The stranger is greeted and brought into its life, and those in need are heard and responded to in the name of Jesus Christ.


## Proper 18, Year C (The Sunday closest to September 7)
Lections: Deuteronomy 30:15-20; Psalm 1; Philemon 1-20; Luke 14:25-33

### Theme of the lections
Counting the cost of discipleship.
- ♦ *Epistle:* Paul asks for the release of a slave.

### Phrases for highlighting and memorization
- ♦ "Choose life so that you and your descendants may live. (Deut. 30:19b)
- ♦ "For the LORD knows the way of the righteous, but the way of the wicked is doomed." (Psalm 1:6)
- ♦ "I am appealing to you for my child, Onesimus, whose father I have become during my imprisonment." (Philemon 10)
- ♦ "Whoever does not carry the cross and follow me cannot be my disciple." (Luke 14:27)

### Key words, ideas, and concepts to explore
- ♦ commandments;
- ♦ "choose life";
- ♦ discipleship;
- ♦ bearing the cross;

• This week Paul's brief letter to Philemon is read. Discuss the background of the letter.

### Formation in baptismal discipleship
Christians must become aware of the radical nature of discipleship. "Bearing the cross" means bearing the pain of injustice and suffering that is so evident in the world. The church and individual Christians are called to be involved in the struggles for wholeness and justice.

## Proper 19, Year C (The Sunday closest to September 14)
Lections: Exodus 32:1, 7-14; Psalm 51:1-11; 1 Timothy 1:12-17; Luke 15:1-10

### Theme of the lections
Jesus seeks out the lost sinners and rejoices at finding them.

### Phrases for highlighting and memorization
• "And the LORD changed his mind about the disaster that he planned to bring on his people." (Exod. 32:14)
• "Have mercy on me, O God, according to your loving-kindness; in your great compassion blot out my offenses." (Psalm 51:1)
• "The saying is sure and worthy of full acceptance, that Christ Jesus came into the world to save sinners—of whom I am the foremost." (1 Tim. 1:15)
• "Just so, I tell you, there will be more joy in heaven over one sinner who repents than over ninety-nine righteous persons who need no repentance." (Luke 15:7)

### Key words, ideas, and concepts to explore
• grace;
• mercy;
• forgiveness;
• Pharisees and scribes;
• Today begins a seven-week reading of 1 and 2 Timothy. Introduce the two epistles, along with Titus. The three epistles together are called the "pastoral epistles" because they deal with pastoral oversight of the New Testament church.

### Stories to tell
- ◆ The golden calf from Exodus;
- ◆ The parables of the lost sheep and the lost coin.

### Christian practice and liturgical tradition
- ◆ The Timothy text quoted above are included in the "comfortable words" following the absolution in Rite I (BCP 332).

### Formation in baptismal discipleship
The congregation engages in evangelism not merely to draw new members into the church, but to reach out to those burdened with their own sense of sin and alienation.


## Proper 20, Year C (The Sunday closest to September 21)
Lections: Amos 8:4-7 (8-12); Psalm 138; 1 Timothy 2:1-8; Luke 16:1-13

### Theme of the lections
Living in preparation for the judgment that is coming. (The parable heard in the gospel this week seems to praise the steward's dishonesty—read the parable with Jesus' sense of humor in mind. The dishonest steward is better prepared than Jesus' disciples!)
- ◆ *Epistle:* A call for the church to pray for the world.

### Phrases for highlighting and memorization
- ◆ "The LORD has sworn by the pride of Jacob: Surely I will never forget any of their deeds." (Amos 8:7)
- ◆ "Though the LORD be high, he cares for the lowly; he perceives the haughty from afar." (Psalm 138:7)
- ◆ "First of all, then, I urge that supplications, prayers, intercessions, and thanksgivings be made for everyone." (1 Tim. 2:1)
- ◆ "So he summoned him and said to him, 'What is this that I hear about you? Give me an accounting of your management, because you cannot be my manager any longer.'" (Luke 16:2)

### Key words, ideas, and concepts to explore
- ◆ intercessory prayer;
- ◆ nature of parables;
- ◆ steward or manager;

- living in readiness for judgment;
- stewardship.

### Stories to tell
- The parable of the dishonest steward.

### Christian practice and liturgical tradition
- The rubrics on page 383 of *The Book of Common Prayer* set forth the topics for intercessory prayer. The church must pray for "the Nation and all in authority," "the welfare of the world" and other people, places, and institutions each time we gather to celebrate the eucharist.

### Formation in baptismal discipleship
Intercessory prayer for the church and for the world must inform the life of the congregation. The church prays through its acts of healing and justice as well as through its words.


## Proper 21, Year C (The Sunday closest to September 28)
Lections: Amos 6:1-7; Psalm 146:4-9; 1 Timothy 6:11-19; Luke 16:19-31

### Theme of the lections
God judges those who neglect the poor and suffering.

### Phrases for highlighting and memorization
- "Alas for those who lie on beds of ivory, and lounge on their couches, and eat lambs from the flock, and calves from the stall...but are not grieved over the ruin of Joseph!" (Amos 6:4, 6b)
- "The LORD loves the righteous; the LORD cares for the stranger; he sustains the orphan and widow, but frustrates the way of the wicked." (Psalm 146:8)
- "As for those who in the present age are rich, command them not to be haughty, or to set their hopes on the uncertainty of riches, but rather on God who richly provides us with everything for our enjoyment." (1 Tim. 6:17)
- "But Abraham said, 'Child, remember that during your lifetime you received your good things, and Lazarus in like manner evil things; but now he is comforted here, and you are in agony.'" (Luke 16:25)

### Key words, ideas, and concepts to explore
- awareness of those who suffer from sickness, hunger, oppression;
- seeking Christ in serving those in need;
- social justice;
- warning to the wealthy.

### Stories to tell
- The story of the rich man and Lazarus.

### Christian practice and liturgical tradition
- The Baptismal Covenant calls each Christian to be aware of suffering and injustice:

  *Will you seek and serve Christ in all persons, loving your neighbor as yourself?...Will you strive for justice and peace among all people, and respect the dignity of every human being?* (BCP 305)

### Formation in baptismal discipleship
The congregation must constantly ask, who is the Lazarus at our gate, and how can we respond?


## Proper 22, Year C (The Sunday closest to October 5)
Lections: Habakkuk 1:1-6(7-11)12-13; 2:1-4; Psalm 37:3-10; 2 Timothy 1:(1-5)6-14; Luke 17:5-10

### Theme of the lections
Living in faith that God will act with justice and healing for the people.
- *Epistle:* The opening words of 2 Timothy praise the faithful leader, Timothy.

### Phrases for highlighting and memorization
- "For there is still a vision for the appointed time; it speaks of the end, and does not lie. If it seems to tarry, wait for it; it will surely come, it will not delay." (Habakkuk 2:3)
- "Commit your way to the LORD and put your trust in him, and he will bring it to pass." (Psalm 37:5)
- "I am reminded of your sincere faith." (2 Tim. 1:5a)

- "If you had faith the size of a mustard seed, you could say to this mulberry tree, 'Be uprooted and planted in the sea,' and it would obey you." (Luke 17:6)

### Key words, ideas and concepts to explore
- the role of watchman and messenger;
- faith;
- visions;
- pastoral epistles (see Proper 19, Year C);
- prayer.

### Christian practice and liturgical tradition
- The ringing of church bells reflects the role of the watchman on the tower walls. Bells have been rung over the generations to warn of impending danger and to announce good news to the people.

### Formation in baptismal discipleship
A role of the church and the individual Christian in society is to serve as a watchtower. The church is to call out and warn society when it perceives evil and destructive practices undermining the life of the people.

## Proper 23, Year C (The Sunday closest to October 12)
Lections: Ruth 1:1(1-7) 8-19a; Psalm 113; 2 Timothy 2:(3-7) 8-15; Luke 17:11-19

### Theme of the lections
The faithfulness of those outside conventional society.
- *Epistle:* God is faithful. That is the word that must be proclaimed.

### Phrases for highlighting and memorization
- "Where you go, I will go; Where you lodge, I will lodge; your people shall be my people, and your God my God." (Ruth 1:16b)
- "He takes up the weak out of the dust and lifts up the poor from the ashes." (Psalm 113:6)
- "The saying is sure: If we have died with him, we will also live with him." (2 Tim. 2:11)
- "Then one of them, when he saw that he was healed, turned back, praising God with a loud voice." (Luke 17:15)

*Key words, ideas, and concepts to explore*
- word of God;
- salvation;
- eternal glory;
- Ruth, the great-grandmother of King David named in Matthew's genealogy of Jesus.

*Stories to tell*
- The story of Ruth and Naomi.

*Christian practice and liturgical tradition*
- Praise is an integral part of Christian worship, and the regular recitation of the psalms is one of the most ancient forms of praise.

*Formation in baptismal discipleship*
The congregation's prayers always include praise and thanksgiving. We become increasingly aware of God's power as we express thanks for what is happening in our lives and in the world.

## Proper 24, Year C (The Sunday closest to October 19)
Lections: Genesis 32:3-8, 22-30; Psalm 121; 2 Timothy 3:14–4:5; Luke 18:1-8a

*Theme of the lections*
Because God loves us, it is all right to "pester" God with our prayers and petitions.
- *Epistle:* Instructions to early church leaders: preach, teach, and live the faith.

*Phrases for highlighting and memorization*
- "But Jacob said, 'I will not let you go, unless you bless me.'" (Gen. 32:26b)
- "My help comes from the LORD, the maker of heaven and earth." (Psalm 121:2)
- "All scripture is inspired by God and is useful for teaching, for reproof, for correction, and for training in righteousness, so that everyone who belongs to God may be proficient, equipped for every good work." (2 Tim. 3:16-17)

◆ "Will not God grant justice to his chosen ones who cry to him day and night? Will he delay long in helping them?" (Luke 18:7)

### Key words, ideas, and concepts to explore
- ◆ blessing;
- ◆ petition;
- ◆ fervent prayer;
- ◆ role of scripture;
- ◆ scripture as inspired.

### Stories to tell
- ◆ The story of Jacob's struggle with the angel.

### Christian practice and liturgical tradition
- ◆ Scripture is read at every service of worship "for teaching, for reproof, for correction, and for training in righteousness" (2 Tim. 3:16).
- ◆ The service of Evening Prayer opens with the words of Psalm 70:1: "O God, make speed to save us. O Lord, make haste to help us" (BCP 117). In these and many other prayers we cry out to God for help and blessing.

### Formation in baptismal discipleship
Scripture must be at the heart of every aspect of congregational life. Dialogue about and study of the scriptures needs to be an integral part of meetings, educational events, and times of discernment.


## Proper 25, Year C (The Sunday closest to October 26)
Lections: Jeremiah 14:(1-6)7-10, 19-22; Psalm 84:1-6; 2 Timothy 4:6-8, 16-18; Luke 18:9-14

### Theme of the lections
The proper attitude to approach God in prayer.
- ◆ *Epistle:* Paul's faith in proclaiming the gospel is remembered.

### Phrases for highlighting and memorization
- ◆ "We acknowledge our wickedness, O LORD, the iniquity of our ancestors, for we have sinned against you." (Jer. 14:20)

- "Happy are they who dwell in your house! they will always be praising you." (Psalm 84:3)
- "I have fought the good fight, I have finished the race, I have kept the faith." (2 Tim. 4:7)
- "I tell you, this man went down to his home justified rather than the other; for all who exalt themselves will be humbled, but all who humble themselves will be exalted." (Luke 18:14)

### Key words, ideas, and concepts to explore
- "that Day" (the day of Christ's return, judgment day, the Day of the Lord);
- prayer;
- Pharisees and tax collectors;
- sinner.

### Christian practice and liturgical tradition
- Confession and penitence are a part of every worship service. Even when there is not a specific prayer of confession at the service, the eucharistic prayers and other prayers of the Prayer Book include an acknowledgment of sin.
- The customs associated with Lent and Holy Week provide a time for the acknowledgment of sin and the need for repentance.

### Formation in baptismal discipleship
Congregational life is balanced between joy and praise on the one hand and a constant awareness of the need for repentance and renewal on the other. The congregation lives in the light of the coming day of judgment.

## Proper 26, Year C (The Sunday closest to November 2)
Lections: Isaiah 1:10-20; Psalm 32:1-8; 2 Thessalonians 1:1-5(6-10)11-12; Luke 19:1-10

### Theme of the lections
The covenant demands justice. Without justice, praise and sacrifice are empty acts that do not make God's people righteous.
- *Epistle:* Christ is to be glorified through the witness of the church.

### Phrases for highlighting and memorization

- "Learn to do good; seek justice, rescue the oppressed, defend the orphan, plead for the widow." (Isa. 1:17)
- "Happy are they whose transgressions are forgiven, and whose sin is put away!" (Psalm 32:1)
- "To this end we always pray for you, asking that our God will make you worthy of his call and will fulfill by his power every good resolve and work of faith, so that the name of our Lord Jesus may be glorified in you, and you in him, according to the grace of our God and the Lord Jesus Christ." (2 Thess. 1:11-12)
- "For the Son of Man came to seek out and to save the lost." (Luke 19:10)

### Key words, ideas, and concepts to explore

- "worthy of [God's] call";
- tax collectors;
- temple practices;
- justice as a right response to God.

### Stories to tell

- The story of Zacchaeus.

### Christian practice and liturgical tradition

- The Baptismal Covenant demands that the Christian be guided by the biblical call for justice.

### Formation in baptismal discipleship

The Isaiah text quoted above shapes the life of a congregation that is serious about being formed by the Baptismal Covenant.


## Proper 27, Year C (The Sunday closest to November 9)

Lections: Job 19:23-27a; Psalm 17:1-8; 2 Thessalonians 2:13–3:5; Luke 20:27 (28-33) 34-38

### Theme of the lections

The resurrection of the dead is proclaimed.

(Note: The themes of the season of Advent begin to be expressed this week, offering an opportunity to explore the rich heritage of Advent.)

• *Epistle:* The church is the "first fruits" of God's salvation revealed in Christ.

### Phrases for highlighting and memorization

• "For I know that my Redeemer lives, and that at the last he will stand upon the earth." (Job 19:25)
• "Let my vindication come forth from your presence; let your eyes be fixed on justice." (Psalm 17:2)
• "But we must always give thanks to God for you, brothers and sisters beloved by the Lord, because God chose you as the first fruits for salvation through sanctification by the Spirit and through belief in the truth." (2 Thess. 2:13)
• "Now he is God not of the dead, but of the living; for to him all of them are alive." (Luke 20:38)

### Key words, ideas, and concepts to explore

• first fruits;
• resurrection;
• redeemer;
• Sadducees.

### Christian practice and liturgical tradition

• The Apostles' Creed and the Nicene Creed affirm the resurrection of the dead and the final judgment: "He will come again in glory to judge the living and the dead, and his kingdom will have no end" (BCP 359).
• "The Christian Hope" section of An Outline of the Faith (BCP 861-862) discusses the final things.
• The joy of the resurrection is reflected in the traditions of Christian burial. See the rubric that begins, "The liturgy for the dead is an Easter liturgy. It finds all its meaning in the resurrection. Because Jesus was raised from the dead, we, too, shall be raised" (BCP 507).

### Formation in baptismal discipleship

The congregation lives in the light of the resurrection and the final judgment. Hope and judgment characterize the outlook of the church as it proclaims Christ to the world.

## Proper 28, Year C (The Sunday closest to November 16)

Lections: Malachi 3:13–4:2a, 5-6; Psalm 98:5-10; 2 Thessalonians 3:6-13; Luke 21:5-19

### Theme of the lections

The coming day of glory and judgment is ushered in by a time of frightening upheaval and persecution.

### Phrases for highlighting and memorization

- "Lo, I will send you the prophet Elijah before the great and terrible day of the LORD comes. He will turn the hearts of parents to their children and the hearts of children to their parents, so that I will not come and strike the land with a curse." (Mal. 4:5-6)
- "In righteousness shall he judge the world and the peoples with equity." (Psalm 98:10)
- "Now we command you, beloved, in the name of our Lord Jesus Christ, to keep away from believers who are living in idleness and not according to the tradition that they received from us." (2 Thess. 3:6)
- "You will be hated by all because of my name. But not a hair of your head will perish. By your endurance you will gain your souls." (Luke 21:17-19)

### Key words, ideas, and concepts to explore

- Elijah as prophet and precursor of the day of the Lord;
- the coming of the Lord;
- judgment day.

### Christian practice and liturgical tradition

See Proper 27, Year C, as well as general remarks in the chapter concerning the season of Advent.

### Formation in baptismal discipleship

See Proper 27, Year C, as well as general remarks in the chapter concerning the season of Advent.

## Proper 29, Year C (The Sunday closest to November 23)

Lections: Jeremiah 23:1-6; Psalm 46; Colossians 1:11-20; Luke 23:35-43 or Luke 19:29-38

### Theme of the lections

This day is often referred to as Christ the King, or the Reign of Christ, Sunday. Christ's sovereignty is the major theme in the lections for all three years.

(Note: Luke 19:29-38, Jesus' triumphal entry into Jerusalem, is an alternative gospel lection. This option also reflects the theme of Christ the King with its clear allusion to Zechariah 9:9: "Lo, your king comes to you; triumphant and victorious is he, humble and riding on a donkey, on a colt, the foal of a donkey.")

### Phrases for highlighting and memorization

- "Then I myself will gather the remnant of my flock out of all the lands where I have driven them, and I will bring them back to their fold, and they shall be fruitful and multiply." (Jer. 23:3)
- "Be still, then, and know that I am God; I will be exalted among the nations; I will be exalted in the earth." (Psalm 46:11)
- "He is the image of the invisible God, the firstborn of all creation; for in him all things in heaven and on earth were created, things visible and invisible, whether thrones or dominions or rulers or powers—all things have been created through him and for him." (Col. 1:15-16)
- "Then he said, 'Jesus, remember me when you come into your kingdom.' He replied, 'Truly I tell you, today you will be with me in Paradise.'" (Luke 23:42-43)

### Key words, ideas, and concepts to explore

- Christ as king or sovereign;
- the work of a shepherd;
- firstborn of all creation;
- Paradise.

### Christian practice and liturgical tradition

- Some of the traditions associated with worship in the Episcopal Church have their origins in the royal court: for example, purple, the color for Advent and Lent, was the color associated with royalty and became linked to the coming of Christ as king.

* The psalms and prayers of the church are filled with imagery of the ruler.

### Formation in baptismal discipleship

"Jesus is Lord" (the earliest Christian creed) means that Jesus stands above all other earthly power and authority. All through history and into the present moment, choosing God above earthly authority has caused persecution and conflict in the life of the church. The congregation and wider church must witness always to the authority of Jesus Christ, realizing that there will be times when conflict will be the direct result of such a witness.

# *Appendix*

## Concerning the Learning Process

Christ's promise to be present when two or three are gathered together in his name (Matt. 18:20) applies to education as well as prayer. The minute we sit down together, we are involved in education; every encounter, whether planned or unplanned, is an opportunity to teach and to learn. Creative and thoughtful planning, however, can enhance the process of learning.

Whenever we start to plan we must be in touch with others, asking if our ideas fit within the overall educational goals of the congregation. Sharing with one another in God's presence produces a synergy of ideas; choosing together among such ideas results in smoother, clearer, and more creative planning; seeking to fill in gaps and to avoid disjointed activities makes for a more cohesive and complete educational program. Whether our colleagues are those working at our side or the far-off writers of books to which we turn, we are never alone in the task of education.

### Planning an Educational Offering
### The Setting
Ask the questions: *Who? Where? When?*

* Who will be there? Whom do we hope to include? Although "education is for everyone," we must be aware of the needs of each specific group of learners.
* Where will it be? What space is available? In what places can learning occur? Recognize that learning can happen at all sorts of occasions (teenagers serving a parish supper, a baptism, vestry planning time, stewardship programs). Comfortable space, lighting, and decor help set the atmosphere but are secondary to the people involved and to the message.

◆ What time is available? What time span is needed? Part of an hour? an evening? a weekend? Perhaps only a few minutes, recurring daily? a series of several weeks? a year-long event? A wide variety of time and space could be considered, but the choice must be right for the group and the topic. Examine and reexamine the situation over time.

### The Purpose/Objectives
Ask the questions: *What do we hope to accomplish? Why are we doing it?*

◆ Develop a purpose statement for the session or program that answers these two questions, such as "To do *something* in order that *something* might happen." Be specific as to what you are going to do and what you hope will happen.

◆ List the objectives you hope to accomplish. Objectives should be attainable and measurable.

◆ To avoid the frustration of an incomplete task, remember that the briefer the time available, the more pointed the focus must be.

### The Leading Theme
Ask the question: *About what main idea are we concerned?*

◆ Considering a common theme can give unity and continuity to a congregation's several programs. Be sure the theme is inclusive enough and part of the church's mission.

◆ Looking at an idea within a theme from several viewpoints, in a variety of ways, gives unexpected insights and understandings.

◆ It is not necessary to teach all there is to know about a theme at one time. Search out the themes within themes within themes. Focus on one point; then, God willing, tomorrow and next year will bring more opportunities.

◆ The church year provides a framework of themes, and the catechism in *The Book of Common Prayer* organizes the Outline of the Faith into eighteen topics. (See "A Seasonal Guide to An Outline of the Faith" later in this chapter for further ideas.)

### The Ways and Means
Ask the questions: *How will we learn? What are the alternatives? What are the resources available?*

◆ Remember that "resources" are people and places, as well as books and activities.

- Explore different ways of learning: lecturing or reading aloud are often the least effective modes of teaching. Try reading together, viewing pictures and slides, doing skits and field trips. Reflecting upon first-hand experience is often the most valuable way to learn.
- A change of pace stimulates imagination and avoids overworking any one sort of activity.

*Planning the Learning Event*

Ask the questions: *Which activity will we choose? What are the learners going to do?*

- Activities should actively involve most learners and call for creativity by the learners.
- Each activity should contribute directly to the focus and be appropriate to the age and skills of the learners.
- Choose activities that the leader has confidence in doing.
- Activities should fit into the time and space allowed.

*The Procedure*

Ask the questions: *Who will do what? What is the schedule? Who has what responsibilities, before and during the event?*

- Stages to a learning event include:

    *Launching*—mark the beginning, clarify the purpose, provide continuity with what has been done before.

    *Presentation*—may be done by teachers or by others.

    *Exploration*—should always be done by the learners.

    *Creative Response*—teachers should encourage learners to risk trying new things and responding in new ways.

    *Conclusion*—may give carry-over, link to next occasion, or be a "cliff-hanger," but be aware that the same people may not be in attendance each time the group meets.

- Being aware of how long each activity should take helps avoid interruption or an unrealistic schedule.
- The teacher needs to know what the logical next step is and to be prepared to move on to a parallel activity, further exploration, or to summary reflection.
- The teacher should keep an overall time scheme in mind, yet remain flexible to extend or cut short the allotted time as responses require. Knowing the focus will help avoid being sidetracked while still acknowledging concerns and interests of the group.

- To backtrack or repeat simply for those who were absent previously denies the work of those who were present. If necessary, include latecomers briefly by having learners review for them.
- Responsibilities are best designated and shared as widely as possible by all those involved.

*The Evaluation*

Ask the question: *How will we know we have reached our objectives?*

- Evaluation is a crucial aspect of any learning event. Evaluation enables us to learn from both our successes and our failures. As soon after the event as possible, stop to review what you did and how you did it.
- Take a short time at the end of a session to get the evaluation of the participants. Youth or adult participants can respond to a written evaluation form; children can be asked questions informally as you are wrapping up a session or after a session is over. The following are examples of the kinds of questions you may want to ask.

   —Our purpose for offering this program was [state the purpose]. How has this purpose been accomplished or not accomplished for you?

   —What in this program was most meaningful to you? least meaningful?

   —If we could do this program again, what would you change? add? leave out?

   —What effect will this program have on you in the future? (Frame this question to fit your purpose statement. For example, if you have just offered a course on world hunger, ask how it will affect the participants' response to the crisis.)

- As part of your evaluation, analyze all the informal and formal sources of data available to you.

   —Think about how you and the participants felt about the session.

   —The "body language" of the participants can tell you more about how involved they felt during the session.

   —Attendance may be controlled by outside circumstances, but people will find ways to attend programs that are really important to them.

   —Where are the handouts and artwork done by the participants? If you find "take home" material left in the pew, take note: their impact probably was not felt.

—Check with parents: what do their children talk about on the way home from church?

—What long-term effects do you see from the program? Are people who were considered "outsiders" signing up to become acolytes or task force members? If so, that is positive feedback for your planning group.

### The Roles of Teachers and Learners

The role of the learner—one on a quest—is to ask questions, and one of the teacher's responsibilities is to use questions carefully to stimulate and encourage the learner's reflection. The teacher must be a questioner as well, and certainly is in a position to accomplish the greatest learning. On the other hand, the role of the teacher *cannot* be that of someone with all the answers. Many people are reluctant to volunteer as teachers because they feel they "don't know enough," when actually the chief requirement is a willingness to search, meanwhile enabling and organizing the journey that the whole group takes together as co-learners.

*The Teacher is...*
- *A listener* who is attentive enough to hear what the learners say; who is aware of what is unsaid; who responds without judgments that stifle; and who knows how to wait upon God.
- *A translator* who puts the words of the church into language that is understandable and images that are recognizable to the learners. "What is the meaning?" is the foremost question.
- *A custom designer* who tailors the curriculum for a specific moment to fit a specific group of learners—by awareness of their interests, skills, and experiences, and by planning and organizing their time together.
- *A pacesetter* who provides a setting and an opportunity to learn within a trusting and respecting community of explorers that cares for and accepts one another; who presents something to pique the learners' curiosity and stir up their questions.

*Questions are Useful...*
- *For information* to recall specific facts, to seek data, or to determine what has been understood. Some questions require correct answers, although the closed nature of such answers tends to limit discussion.

At the same time, too many of such questions create a testing, competitive atmosphere where learners can be put on the defensive.

♦ *For analysis* to stimulate thinking further, to lead to conjectures, to dig for reasons, to evaluate a situation. These questions offer the possibility of several responses. Additional questions may follow naturally. "Why...?" and "What do you think...?" can initiate them. But if thoughts are belittled, judged, or contradicted by others in group, open expression becomes reluctant or stifled.

♦ *For personal reactions* to identify with, or to relate something to one's own life, as guides to discover values, to make decisions, to reflect. Answers will be interpretive, and might include "What would you have done...?", or "When have you ever felt...?" But it should be noted that many such questions do not contribute automatically to the learnings of the whole group. To avoid invasion of privacy, reserve the learner's right to delay an answer or to be silent.

## Suggested References and Resources

### Liturgy and Worship

♦ *The Book of Occasional Services.* New York: Church Hymnal Corporation.

♦ *Lesser Feasts and Fasts.* New York: Church Hymnal Corporation.[1]

♦ Kucharski, Joseph, ed. *The Episcopal Musician's Handbook.* Sauk Center, Minn.: Handbook Foundation.

♦ *The Hymnal Companion.* New York: Church Hymnal Corporation, 1996. (A four-volume set.)

♦ *Lift Every Voice and Sing II: An African American Hymnal.* New York: Church Hymnal Corporation, 1993.

♦ MacLean, Paul and Cowling, Douglas. *Sharing the Banquet: Liturgical Renewal in your Parish.* Toronto: Anglican Book Centre, 1993. (Available through Forward Movement.)

♦ Micks, Marianne H. *Deep Waters: An Introduction to Baptism.* Cambridge, Mass.: Cowley Publications, 1996.

♦ Micks, Marianne H. *Loving the Questions: An Exploration of the Nicene Creed.* Cambridge, Mass.: Cowley Publications, 1993.

---

1 New editions of *The Book of Occasional Services* and *Lesser Feasts and Fasts* are published after each General Convention to reflect changes brought about by Convention actions.

◆ Nelson, Gertrud Mueller. *To Dance with God: Family Ritual and Community Celebration.* New York: Paulist Press, 1986.

◆ O'Driscoll, Herbert. *For All the Saints: Homilies for Saints' and Holy Days.* Cambridge, Mass.: Cowley Publications, 1995.

◆ O'Driscoll, Herbert. *Prayers for the Breaking of Bread: Meditations on the Collects of the Church Year.* Cambridge, Mass.: Cowley Publications, 1991.

◆ Plater, Ormonde. *Intercession: A Theological and Practical Guide.* Cambridge, Mass.: Cowley Publications, 1995.

◆ Ramshaw, Gail, ed. *Intercessions for the Christian People.* Collegeville, Minn.: Liturgical Press, 1988. (Prayers of the People reflecting the themes of the propers are offered for every Sunday and Holy Day in the three-year lectionary.)

◆ Stevick, Daniel B. *Baptismal Moments; Baptismal Meanings.* New York: Church Hymnal Corporation, 1987.

◆ Stevick, Daniel B. *The Crafting of Liturgy.* New York: Church Hymnal Corporation, 1990.

◆ Stuhlman, Byron David. *Redeeming the Time: An Historical and Theological Study of the Church's Rule of Prayer and the Regular Services of the Church.* New York: Church Hymnal Corporation, 1992.

◆ Van Olst, E. H. *The Bible and Liturgy.* Grand Rapids, Mich.: William B. Eerdmans, 1991.

◆ Wainwright, Geoffrey. *Doxology: The Praise of God in Worship, Doctrine and Life.* New York: Oxford University Press, 1980.

◆ Westerhoff, Caroline. *Calling: A Song for the Baptized.* Cambridge, Mass.: Cowley Publications, 1994. (Reflections on the meaning of baptism, using the Baptismal Covenant as a framework.)

## The Lectionary

◆ Borsch, Frederick Houk. *Introducing the Lessons of the Church Year.* Valley Forge, Penn.: Trinity Press International, 1991.

◆ Daw, Carl P., ed. *Breaking the Word: Essays on the Liturgical Dimensions of Preaching.* New York: Church Hymnal Corporation, 1994.

◆ *HarperCollins Study Bible, with the Apocryphal/Deuterocanonical Books, New Revised Standard Version.* New York: HarperCollins, 1993.

◆ *The New Oxford Annotated Bible with the Aprocrypha, New Revised Standard Version.* New York: Oxford University Press, 1994.

- *The Revised Common Lectionary.* Nashville, Tenn.: Abingdon Press, 1992.
- Russell, Joseph P. *Sharing Our Biblical Story: A Guide to Using Liturgical Readings at the Core of Church and Family Education, revised edition.* Wilton, Conn.: Morehouse-Barlow, 1988.
- *Texts for Preaching: A Lectionary Commentary Based on the NRSV.* Louisville, Ky.: Westminster/John Knox Press, 1995. (Separate volumes are available for Years A, B, and C.)

### Learning Resources

- Berryman, Jerome W. *Godly Play: An Imaginative Approach to Religious Education.* Minneapolis, Minn.: Augsburg, 1991.
- *Called to Teach and Learn: A Catechetical Guide for the Episcopal Church.* New York: The Domestic and Foreign Missionary Society, PECUSA, 1994.
- *The Catechumenal Process: Adult Initiation and Formation for Christian Life and Ministry.* New York: Church Hymnal Corporation, 1990.
- *In Dialogue with Scripture: An Episcopal Guide to Studying the Bible.* New York: The Episcopal Church Center, n.d.[2]
- Merriman, Michael W., ed. *The Baptismal Mystery and the Catechumenate.* New York: Church Hymnal Corporation, 1990.
- Pritchard, Gretchen Wolff. *Offering the Gospel to Children.* Cambridge, Mass.: Cowley Publications, 1992.
- Stephens, Lois A., with Grenz, Linda L., ed. *I Love to Tell the Story: An Episcopal Handbook on Christian Education.* Center for Christian Formation, 420 East 51st Street, New York, New York 10022.
- Westerhoff, John H., III, and Williamon, William H. *Liturgy and Learning Through the Life Cycle.* Akron, Ohio: Order of St. Luke Publications, 1994.
- Westerhoff, John H., III, *Will Our Children Have Faith?* San Francisco: HarperSanFrancisco, 1976.

---

2   Orders for Episcopal Church Center resources can be placed with Episcopal Parishes Resources, P. O. Box 269, William Penn Annex, Philadelphia, PA, 19105-0269, 1-800-903-5544. Catalogs are available.

"An Outline of the Faith commonly called the Catechism" (BCP 845-862) provides a brief review of the church's teaching that can be used as an outline for instruction. The following pages suggest links between the church's calendar of seasons and feast days and the various sections of the catechism that might be incorporated into an educational program, sermon, or discussion group offered during that season.

### Advent

◆ *The Old Covenant (BCP 846-847)*
    The church looks back to the old covenant during Advent in order to understand the future promise of God.
◆ *God the Son (BCP 849-850)*
    Advent is a time of looking for Christ to come again.
◆ *The Christian Hope (BCP 861-862)*
    Advent points ahead to Christ's coming again and shares the vision of God's coming reign.

### Christmas

◆ *God the Son (BCP 849-850)*
    Christmas celebrates the incarnation of God in Jesus.
◆ *The New Covenant (BCP 850-851)*
    Christmas proclaims that all people could know God "in the flesh" in Jesus. The New Covenant was established out of that encounter of "knowing the Lord" (Jeremiah 31:31-34).

### Epiphany

◆ *The Ministry (BCP 855-856)*
    Epiphany and the Sundays after the Epiphany focus on the calling of the disciples and the nature of discipleship.
◆ *Holy Baptism (BCP 858-859)*
    One of the four "especially appropriate" times for baptism is Epiphany 1, the feast recalling the baptism of Jesus.

### Lent

◆ *Human Nature (BCP 845)*
    Lent helps us see who we are in light of the gospel.

- *The Ten Commandments (BCP 847-848)*

  Lent focuses on the covenant made at baptism and renewed at every celebration of the Holy Eucharist. The Penitential Order often used during this season may include the reading of the Decalogue (BCP 317-318/350).
- *Sin and Redemption (BCP 848-849)*

  Lent deals directly with sin and redemption.
- *God the Son (BCP 849-850)*

  Lent reminds us of the role of Christ in bringing salvation.
- *The Holy Scriptures (BCP 853-854)*

  The lectionary readings during Lent provide a sweep of the biblical story recalled at the Easter Vigil.
- *Holy Baptism (BCP 858-859)*

  Lent is a season of preparation for baptisms at the Easter Vigil.
- *Other Sacramental Rites (BCP 860-861)*

  The rite of the Reconciliation of a Penitent (BCP 447-452) is especially appropriate during the Lenten season.

### Holy Week

- *Sin and Redemption (BCP 848-849)*

  Holy Week deals directly with redemption through Christ's death and resurrection.
- *God the Son (BCP 849-850)*

  Holy Week reminds us of the role of Christ in bringing salvation.
- *The Holy Eucharist (BCP 859-860)*

  Maundy Thursday remembers the institution of the Lord's Supper.

### Easter

- *God the Son (BCP 849-850)*

  Easter proclaims Christ's victory even over death.
- *The New Covenant (BCP 850-851)*

  A new covenant people was formed out of the resurrection of Christ.
- *The Holy Spirit (BCP 852-853)*

  The resurrection led to the gift of the Holy Spirit promised by Jesus before his death (John 15).
- *Holy Baptism (BCP 858-859)*

  Baptism into the new covenant of life in Christ is the primary focus of the Easter Vigil. The vigil is one of the four "most appropriate" days for baptisms.

- *The Holy Eucharist (BCP 859-860)*

  Every Sunday is a "little Easter," a day to proclaim that Christ has risen.

- *The Christian Hope (BCP 861-862)*

  Easter expresses the hope of resurrection.

### Ascension Day

- *God the Son (BCP 849-850)*

  The feast of the Ascension points to the eternal role of Christ, seated at the right hand of God.

### The Day of Pentecost

- *The New Covenant (BCP 850-851)*

  The new covenant established in Christ was written on the hearts of the people through the indwelling power of the Holy Spirit.

- *The Holy Spirit (BCP 852-853)*

  The Day of Pentecost marks the gift of the Holy Spirit to the church.

- *The Church (BCP 854-855)*

  On the first Pentecost the church was empowered to act in the name of Christ. This feast day is considered the "birthday" of the church.

- *The Ministry (BCP 855-856)*

  Christians are empowered for ministry by the Holy Spirit.

- *Holy Baptism (BCP 858-859)*

  The Day of Pentecost is one of the four "most appropriate" days for baptism in the church calendar. Pentecost recognizes the empowerment of the Holy Spirit at baptism and confirmation.

### Trinity Sunday

- *God the Father (BCP 846)*

  Trinity Sunday is a time to focus on the Trinity as a way of understanding God. God the Father has traditionally been known as the first person of the Trinity.

- *God the Son (BCP 849-850)*

  Trinity Sunday is a time to focus on the Trinity as a way of understanding God. God the Son has traditionally been known as the second person of the Trinity.

◆ *The Holy Spirit (BCP 852-853)*

Trinity Sunday is a time to focus on the Trinity as a way of understanding God. God the Holy Spirit has traditionally been known as the third person of the Trinity.

◆ *The Creeds (BCP 851-852)*

God the Trinity is described in the creeds of the church, including the Nicene Creed (BCP 326/358), the Apostles' Creed (BCP 53/96), and the Creed of Athanasius (BCP 864).

### The Season after Pentecost

◆ *The Holy Scriptures (BCP 853-854)*

The gospels and epistles are read semi-continuously for half of the year as a way of exploring the New Testament in depth.

◆ *The Ministry (BCP 855-856)*

The lectionary readings during the weeks after Pentecost focus on the ministry of Jesus and the early disciples.

### All Saints' Day

◆ *The New Covenant (BCP 850-851)*

The feast of All Saints recognizes the covenant community in this life and in the age to come.

◆ *The Church (BCP 854-855)*

All Saints' Day celebrates the communion of saints that is the church throughout all ages.

◆ *Holy Baptism (BCP 858-859)*

The feast of All Saints is one of the four "most appropriate" days for baptism in the church calendar. Those who are baptized are welcomed into the communion of the saints.

◆ *The Christian Hope (BCP 861-862)*

All Saints' Day recognizes the hope of life to come in the communion of saints.

### All Days and Seasons

◆ *Prayer and Worship (BCP 856-857)*

Prayer and worship lie at the heart of the Christian faith and life.

◆ *The Sacraments (BCP 857-858)*

The sacraments of God's grace are celebrated and lived out by Christians every day.

◆ *Other Sacramental Rites (BCP 860-861)*

Other sacramental rites celebrated in the Episcopal Church throughout the church year include Confirmation, Ordination, Holy Matrimony, Reconciliation of a Pentitent, and Ministration to the Sick.